PRISONERS OF THE TOWER

The Tower of London as a state prison, 1100–1941

HISTORIC ROYAL PALACES

Sir Thomas More's departure from his daughter, Margaret Roper, by William Frederick Yeames, 1863. The Tower's role as a prison and place of execution has drawn crowds of spectators and visitors for centuries.

Contents

Case studies

Introduction

Prisons and imprisonment

Professor David Wilson
Centre for Criminal Justice Policy and Research, UCE Birmingham

Prisons in modern British society

Prisons are rarely out of the news, whether it be the suicide of a notorious serial killer such as Harold Shipman or the publication of the latest prison numbers, showing that the British penal system has reached a new 'all time high'. In Britain, criminals are imprisoned at a rate greater than any other country in Europe and there are more life sentence prisoners than in the rest of Western Europe combined. Prisons and imprisonment continue to dominate the media, politics and public policy agenda.

Quite simply, for many politicians and members of the public 'prison works', meaning that our prison population continues to grow, despite the costs involved and the reality that most of those who come to be 'banged up' in our 139 gaols – a figure somewhat higher than the number of universities in the country – have not committed violent offences. We know that there is at best a weak relationship between the incarceration rate and the crime rate.

Why have England and Wales become the 'prison capital of Europe' and what is it that we hope to achieve when we lock up the 75,000 people who are currently in our gaols? By knowing more about the path that has been followed over the past two centuries and more, we may begin to understand the system of state imprisonment that the Tower of London once headed and how that world was transformed into our own.

Criminologists suggest that there are four justifications used for imprisoning offenders: incapacitation, retribution, deterrence and rehabilitation. The first of these is of course linked to the 'common sense' reality that if someone is locked up in a prison then they cannot commit further crimes against the public, at least for the duration of their incarceration. So too with retribution. People who have offended deserve to be punished and imprisonment is, of course, the most severe punishment that the state currently has available at its disposal. Until 1965 execution was the most extreme punishment available and many sentences of death were carried out on Tower Hill and within the confines of the Tower of London. Whilst most of us would accept that people who pose a danger to the public deserve to be locked up, at least until that danger subsides, many of those who end up in our gaols do so not because they are potentially a threat to others, but rather because politicians of both major parties want to demonstrate that they are being 'tough' on crime, which is usually code for being 'tough' on offenders.

Again, common sense suggests that imprisoning at the rate that we do acts as a deterrent. If only it was as simple as this then we would have seen a steady decline in the number of offences being committed, and a steady rise in the crime rates of our European neighbours, who use a much lower rate of imprisonment. In reality we see neither effect. Frustratingly, the deterrent effect of the gaol has, at best, only a fleeting basis in reality, most offenders being more deterred by the certainty that they will be

HM Prison Pentonville. There are 139 prisons in England and Wales currently holding some 75,000 people.

caught, rather than the severity of what might happen to them on the occasions that they are. And what of rehabilitation? With the exception of one or two 'therapeutic prisons', no modern British prison is able to demonstrate that being sent there has led to a reduction in criminal behaviour. For the majority of prisoners, prison has the effect of accelerating their offending behaviour, rather than reducing it.

So, if all of this is true, why do we continue to imprison as we do, and why have prison numbers grown to the extent that they have?

Imprisonment in the past

The answers to these questions are deep and complex, but are clearly located in our collective, national history. Indeed, this book provides some of the background to the circumstances that led to one prison, the Tower of London, coming to dominate our social and political consciousness. The Tower has been established as the pre-eminent setting for the means by which the state expressed its disapproval of certain individuals and activities. We need to remind ourselves, however, that the Tower, a state prison for over 800 years, was but one of many gaols, albeit one that has come to dominate the popular imagination.

This popular fascination that we have with gaols is interesting too, but beyond the scope of this introduction. It is worth commenting that the Tower – a prison that has been, to use a modern phrase, 'decommissioned' as a gaol since the Second World War – is still one of the few places of confinement that may be visited by members of the public. For, not only have high prison walls served to keep their inmates inside, but also the public outside – forever held at bay, leaving the average citizen only able to imagine all manner of activities that might be occurring behind the gates and turrets. Prison, even in the modern world, is still shrouded in secrecy.

The Tower acted as a state prison from at least 1100 – when it locked up its first recorded prisoner, Ranulf Flambard – until 1820, and thereafter at times of national emergency, such as when it imprisoned its last two prisoners – Rudolph Hess, Hitler's Deputy Reichsführer, for four days in May 1941, and the spy Josef Jakobs who was shot on 15 August 1941, in the Rifle Range that stood in the Outer Ward. The detailed history of these developments in imprisonment, punishment and execution is set out in the chapters that follow. But what of other London prisons, and when did the state take over complete control of the penal system?

The Tower's penal role for prisoners of state notwithstanding, the state's general interest in prisons and prisoners is a relatively recent phenomenon. Essentially, it can be traced back to the end of the transportation of convicted criminals, first to the Americas – ended by the Declaration of American Independence in 1776 – and thereafter to Botany Bay in Australia in 1857. As a consequence, the state had to become involved with

The male and female wards of the Whitecross Street prison for debtors, London, 1843. Whitecross was closed in 1870 as imprisonment for debt had become rare.

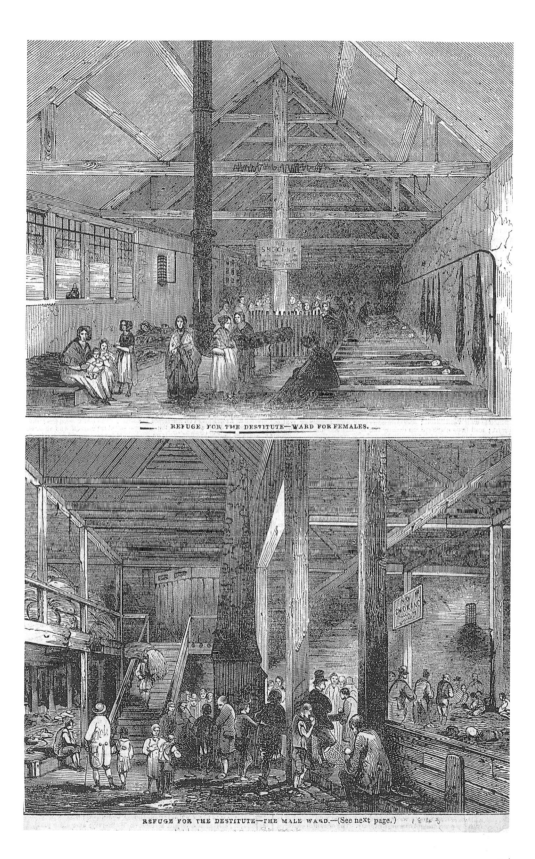

REFUGE FOR THE DESTITUTE—WARD FOR FEMALES.

REFUGE FOR THE DESTITUTE—THE MALE WARD.—(See next page.)

prisoners for longer, not only holding them prior to their trial, but also with what to do with them after they had been sentenced but could no longer be transported, or indeed executed.

Until this time prisons were in effect places that held those people who had been accused of crimes and were awaiting trial, or had been convicted and were awaiting exile or execution, or else they housed debtors. Most local gaols – sometimes known as 'houses of correction', or 'bridewells' – were administered by the county magistrates through private contractors.

Britain's greatest prison reformer – John Howard, a former Sheriff of Bedfordshire (now best known through the Howard League for Penal Reform which is named in his honour) – described in *The State of the Prisons in England and Wales*, published in 1777, how most county gaols were 'filthy, corrupt-ridden and unhealthy'. He drew particular attention to the traditional system by which local gaolers, who received no salary, made their living by selling board and lodgings to the prisoners, with all the potential for corruption that this created. Some prisoners could live comparatively well, in special lodgings within the gaol, buying better food than the average prisoner and having beer and wine, and many were accompanied within the prison by members of their family. Others who could not afford to pay lived in appalling conditions.

John Howard (1726?–90), Britain's greatest prison reformer, by William Daniell after George Dance. Howard himself experienced imprisonment in France in 1756 after the ship he was travelling in was captured by a French privateer.

Marshalsea prison on Borough High Street, Southwark, 1773. In 1738 an anonymous pamphlet described the Marshalsea as 'an old pile most dreadful to the view, Dismal as wormwood or repenting rue'.

Charles Dickens by Herbert Watkins, 1858. Dickens's novel, Little Dorrit (1855–7), was set in the Marshalsea prison where his father, John, was imprisoned in 1824.

Charles Dickens, for example, whose father had been imprisoned in London's Marshalsea prison in February 1824 for debt, found youthful employment in a blacking factory – a set of circumstances that he was later to employ in *David Copperfield*. Dickens used his knowledge of London's prisons and what went on within them most directly in *Little Dorrit*, which he set in the Marshalsea. Amy, the 'Little Dorrit' of the title, who had even been born in the gaol, could move in and out of the prison at will, bringing back with her food and wine.

However, the days of the Marshalsea and the type of internal regime that it operated were already numbered, for as early as 1810, with the establishment of the Holford Committee, central government had begun the process of discussing in earnest what was to be done about prisons and the role that the state should play in the process of imprisonment.

Millbank prison, completed in 1816, was London's largest prison and was used for criminals awaiting transportation or referral.

The Holford Committee recommended – much to the annoyance of Jeremy Bentham, who had designed a prison called the Panopticon, which was rejected by the committee – that a new state penitentiary should be built at Millbank in central London. This was completed in 1816. If we exclude the Tower, Millbank was in effect the first purpose built state prison, to be followed by the opening of the second state penitentiary at Her

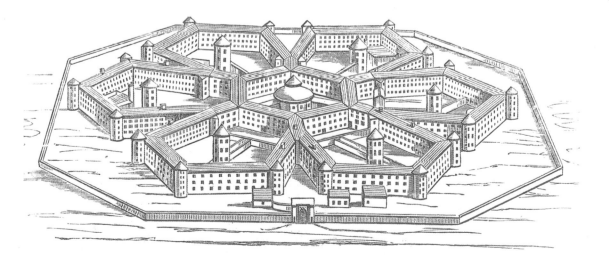

Majesty's Prison Pentonville in 1842. Millbank prison was demolished in 1893; its site is now occupied by the Tate Gallery. Prisons, like workhouses and mental asylums, were among the distinctive local public buildings of the Victorian age, and gaols rose in most parts of the country in the 1850s and 1860s.

During this time, as the state gradually extended its influence over the penal estate, debate raged as to what should happen to prisoners after they had been locked up. Should they be 'silent and separate' from each other, allowed only to reflect on their crimes (in effect being 'penitent'), or should they be encouraged to associate with each other and be given appropriate work? In some ways this debate reflects a more contemporary preoccupation about the purpose of imprisonment, and the role that prison can be expected to play when it imprisons offenders – beyond keeping them in custody. There are still many echoes of that debate today – just as this debate may be altered by public reaction to high profile crimes and notorious criminals, so too did events in the 19th century have a major and long-lasting effect. The 'garrotting panic' of the 1860s (a popular and media-inspired anxiety that newly released prisoners were roaming the streets of London garrotting, or attacking, members of the public by choking them) heavily influenced the type of penal system that was to emerge with the Prison Act of 1877, when the state finally took control of all the country's gaols. By this time, the general revision of the penal code meant that fewer criminals were being sentenced to be executed and the death penalty was reserved for capital murder.

The Prison Act of 1877 transferred responsibility for prisons from the local justices of the peace to the Home Secretary. Administration of the new system was placed in the hands of a Prison Commission, which was asked to reduce costs and establish greater uniformity and efficiency in the running of the penal estate. The first Chairman of the Prison Commission was the hard-line Sir Edmund Du Cane, who wanted imprisonment to be about 'general deterrence' and characterised prison life as being about 'hard labour, hard board and hard fare'. As such, prisoners were largely kept in solitary confinement, were given a standard uniform and were allowed only a regulation diet. They were given work, such as stone breaking, sewing mailbags and picking oakum (removing fibres from old ropes). This demeaning and painful work was described by Oscar Wilde in his great poem *The Ballad of Reading Gaol*:

We tore the tarry rope to shreds
With blunt and bleeding nails;
We rubbed the doors, and scrubbed the floors,
And cleaned the shining rails:
And, rank by rank, we soaped the plank,
And clattered with the pails.

We sewed the sacks, we broke the stones,
We turned the dusty drill:
We banged the tins, and bawled the hymns
And sweated on the mill:
But in the heart of every man
Terror was lying still.

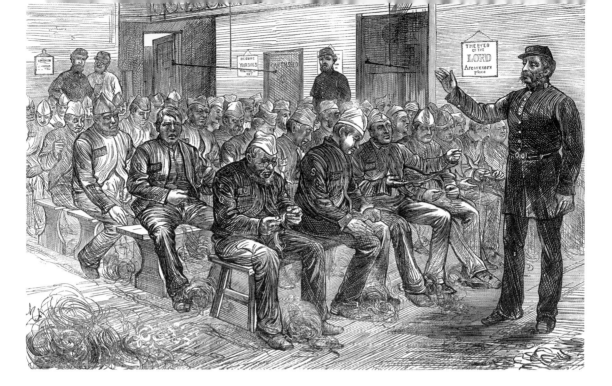

Imprisonment in the 20th century

The type of imprisonment that Wilde so aptly evoked, based as it was on the supposed deterrent effect of incarceration, was replaced in 1898. Attitudes were changing. Arguing that all prisoners were different and that hard labour did not stop prisoners re-offending, the Gladstone Committee recommended in 1895 that prisons should be 'more capable of being adopted to the special cases of individual prisoners' and that prison regimes should 'maintain, stimulate or awaken the higher susceptibilities of prisoners, to develop their moral instincts, to train them in orderly and industrial habits, and wherever possible to turn them out of prison better men and women, both physically and morally, than when they came in'.

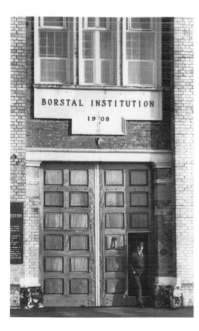

The Prisons Act of 1898 saw hard labour abolished and a classification system introduced for prisoners based on their age, gender and whether or not they were sentenced or awaiting trial. In the decades that followed a special type of prison – known as a borstal – was introduced for young offenders in 1908. In 1910 Winston Churchill, at the time Home Secretary, and himself a former prisoner of war, linked the 'mood and temper of the public in regard to the treatment of crime and criminals' as one of 'the most unfailing tests of the civilization of any country'.

Churchill was not alone in being sceptical about the continued use of prison as a means of dealing with crime. With the development of a probation system for offenders and the imprisonment of largely middle class suffragettes and First World War conscientious objectors, criticism of the penal system reached new highs. As a consequence, the prison population began to drop dramatically. Indeed, in one of the few sustained periods of decarceration in criminological history, the prison population of England and Wales fell from 22,090 in 1908, or 63 prisoners per 100,000 of the general population, to 11,086 in 1938, or just 30 prisoners per 100,000 of the general population.

This decline in the prison population was not sustained after the Second World War when numbers started to increase steadily once again – in contrast to our European neighbours. Indeed, it is tempting to see the differences between British approaches to prisons and those of mainland Europe as linked to differing experiences of war, with those countries that had been invaded by Nazi Germany adopting a much more liberal approach to imprisonment after liberation.

In any event with prison numbers increasing, concerns inevitably re-emerged about the internal running of our prisons, and became focussed on security – especially escapes. For example, in 1946 there had been 864 escapes and attempted escapes, but by 1964 there were 2,090, some very prominent spies and criminals among them. This first 'security crisis' as it has been called, led to the Mountbatten Report of 1966, which recommended that prisoners be divided into four security categories – A (the highest), B, C, D (the lowest). The decision was taken to disperse rather than concentrate Category A prisoners to produce what is now known as the 'high security estate'.

The more recent history of our penal system has remained dominated by disorder – especially riots, and of new security crises. The 1980s road to privatisation in the state sector has been extended to prisons and for the first time since the mid-19th century there are private prisons as well as state prisons once more. The cumulative effect has been to see conditions toughen in our gaols. Allied to more political desires to be 'tough on crime', through, for example, mandatory minimum sentencing, not only have prison numbers continued to rise, but we also seem to have returned to justifying imprisonment on the basis of its general deterrent effect. In short, prison is seen to work, despite all too much evidence to the contrary.

Imprisonment has reflected its era, from the political concerns and cruel punishments that gave the Tower of London its notoriety to the rise of Victorian certainties and 20th-century crises of confidence. The intention of this introduction is to allow you to put your visit to the Tower of London into an overall and more familiar context. The chapters that follow will direct you to more specific information about the workings of the Tower as a prison of the past.

As visitors walk round they might also reflect that whilst the original instruments of torture no longer exist, the prison population of England and Wales is still at an all-time high. And, unlike visitors, the 75,000 who are currently imprisoned cannot leave at the end of the day.

PRISONERS OF THE TOWER

Sent to the Tower

The Tower of London was not built as a prison. Yet ever since its construction by William the Conqueror (1066–87) as a fortress, men and women have been imprisoned there. Some have stayed for only a few days, others for many years. Over the centuries, the Tower was a potent symbol of state authority and an object of fear. Many of those imprisoned were some of the most important figures in English history. Three English queens were executed within its walls, and countless foreign princes and English aristocrats survived or died at the state's pleasure from the 12th to the 18th century. During this period, the Tower became the country's principal 'state' prison for the incarceration of those men and women deemed to be a threat to national security.

However, the story of imprisonment is not simply one of traitors and heroes forced to cower in rat-infested dungeons until their inevitable appointment with the executioner's axe. It is also a tale of luxury, banquets, scientific experiments and great works of literature. Many prisoners did not end their lives there but were released, after a ransom was paid or when they were no longer a threat to the government of the day. It is a remarkably varied story of deposed kings imprisoned alongside ordinary men and women locked up for ordinary crimes. Just as the Tower itself has played many roles throughout its history, so too it has served many purposes as a prison.

The first prisoner arrived at the Tower

Catherine Howard (c1520–42), fifth wife of Henry VIII, by Hans Holbein the Younger. The Queen was executed on Tower Green for high treason on 13 February 1542. She was reportedly so weak she could hardly speak.

The Poems of Charles, Duke of Orleans, c1483. The Duke was captured at the Battle of Agincourt in 1415 and the poetry he composed during his imprisonment was later transcribed into an elaborate manuscript. This illumination provides us with one of the earliest views of the Tower.

on Wednesday 15 August 1100. Ranulf Flambard had been Bishop of Durham and chief tax gatherer for William II (1087–1100). Under the new king, Henry I (1100–35), he was accused of extortion and hauled off to the White Tower in chains. This was a popular move for a new ruler and went down well with taxpayers. Over 800 years later, on 15 August 1941, Josef Jakobs was executed by firing squad at the Tower, having been found guilty of spying for Germany during the Second World War. In between, the Tower has been custodian of kings, queens, priests, Welsh, Scottish, French, German and American prisoners of war, thieves and politicians.

By the Tudor period, the Tower had become the foremost state prison in the country. Those accused of more ordinary crimes were now more usually locked up in other London gaols – like the Newgate and the Fleet. This is what defines the Tower more than anything else as a symbol of state power, and the Tower itself has not

Serving time

Imprisonment at the Tower of London has, over the centuries, varied from the luxurious to the lethal. This might depend on the nature of the prisoner's offence, the instability of the current reign or the status of the prisoner. Some enjoyed particularly comfortable 'imprisonments'. King John Baliol of Scotland spent three years at the Tower in the 13th century, after his capture at the Battle of Dunbar by the English armies of Edward I (1272–1307). He was allowed out hunting and could travel up to 21 miles outside the City of London. According to the accounts submitted by Ralph of Sandwich, then Constable of the Tower, the Scottish king was accompanied by a vast retinue of servants. Room had to be found for two squires, a huntsman, a barber, a chaplain, a chapel clerk and several assistants, two grooms and two chamberlains, a tailor, a laundress, three pages and a pack of two greyhounds and ten hunting dogs. There was also a 'pledge-man' who had to stay behind at the Tower when King John went off hunting.

Another King John, John the Good of France, spent a similarly opulent period at the Tower in 1360. The Tower effectively became the French court in exile and John's attendants included an organist and 'Master John the Fool'. Not all prisoners had the status or importance as a French king of course, and Edward III (1327–77), who was royally entertained by John at a lavish banquet prepared in his own palace at the Tower, expected to recoup the immense expense of the

been reluctant to exploit this. Driven by the need to ensure the obedience of the population, the Tower consciously sought to reinforce its image as unassailable fortress and unbreakable prison. More recently, it has emphasised its gruesome and violent past as a means of attracting visitors.

King John Baliol of Scotland (reigned 1292–6) and his wife. Baliol was imprisoned in the Salt Tower for three years after surrendering his crown to Edward I.

'The Tower of London Hours'. This small devotional book from the second half of the 15th century was owned by a prisoner of the Tower known only as John Lucas of Ashford. The inscriptions at the front of the book record the executions of Sir William Stanley in 1495 and of the Duke of Buckingham in 1521.

Statue of Ranulf Flambard in the grounds of Christchurch Priory, Dorset, where he founded a Norman church in 1094.

Ranulf Flambard, Bishop of Durham (d 1128)

PRISONER: 1100−1

The first high-profile prisoner in the Tower became its first escapee. Ranulf was an ambitious clerk and courtier in the reign of William II. Surnamed *Flambard*, 'the fire-raiser', his voracity as the King's chief tax collector was matched only by his personal greed. Entrusted with raising revenue from the church lands held illegally by the King, he ensured his own elevation to the powerful position of Bishop of Durham.

When Henry I succeeded to the throne, he earned public support by immediately imprisoning the much-hated tax gatherer. Ranulf was led in chains to the Tower to be guarded by the Constable of the Tower, William de Mandeville. The wily Bishop used the cover of the feast of Candlemas (2 February 1101) to effect his escape. As a chronicler writes:

One day a rope was smuggled to him in a gallon of wine. The generous bishop then proceeded to lay on a great banquet, at which his guards ate with him and became intoxicated with all the wine they had consumed. When they were completely drunk and snoring soundly, the bishop produced the rope and tied it to the column which stood in the middle of a window of the tower: holding his pastoral staff with him, he climbed down the rope... His loyal friends and trusted cohorts were waiting in great fear at the foot of the tower, where they had the swiftest horses ready for him...

They made their escape to Normandy to plot the King's overthrow. William de Mandeville was heavily fined for letting him escape. Ranulf, on the other hand, soon returned to the King's favour and lived out the rest of his life, with considerable scandal, in his bishopric.

John II of France (1319–64)

John II of France by an unknown artist, c1360.

PRISONER: 1360

Of all the medieval prisoners in the Tower, most is known about the imprisonment of the French king, John II ('the Good') (1350–64). He was the most important of the many nobles captured by Edward, Prince of Wales ('the Black Prince'), son of Edward III, at the Battle of Poitiers in 1356. After being moved between various locations in England and France, King John finally arrived at the Tower in April 1360 while negotiations for his ransom were being concluded. In preparation for his arrival, Edward III sent orders for the records of

King John being taken prisoner at the Battle of Poitiers in 1356.

Chancery to be moved from the White Tower to make room for the considerable entourage of his 'French adversary'. The London carpenter, Denys le Lombard, was paid to make wooden frames to fit oil-cloth over four windows in the King's chamber.

John the Good stayed in the White Tower in considerable style, treated with all the dignity and consideration that his rank merited. In addition to his own extensive retinue of gentlemen (most of whom were lodged outside the castle in the houses of London citizens), he was accompanied by such diverse figures as his youngest son Philippe (captured with him), the tailor Tassin de Breuil, the secretary Jean le Royer, the *maître d'ôtel* Jean de Dainville, 'Master John the Fool' and the Londoner 'John the Organist'. He arrived with five wagons: one each for him and his son, one for the goods of his chapel, one for John the Fool and one for the kitchen. The organist came later in an additional wagon with his instruments, a man to work the bellows and two servants. Surviving accounts show that King John and his party ate very well indeed. He also spent money on visits to the court at Westminster, to religious houses and local hermitages, shopping expeditions in London and numerous presents to officers at the Tower including constables and sub-constables, guards and porters, chaplains and the lion-keeper.

Once negotiations were completed later in the year, King John held a feast for Edward III and Queen Philippa of Hainault at the Tower at his own expense. His ransom was fixed at the stupendous sum of half a million pounds sterling. The French king, on his word of honour not to violate the treaty, returned home to arrange the collection of the money. He left his second son, the Duke of Anjou, as hostage in Calais. When John the Good discovered Anjou had escaped and unable to raise his ransom, he chivalrously returned to captivity in England, where he died in 1364.

The magnificent fireplace that still survives in the Salt Tower reveals the relative luxury of the accommodation for those imprisoned there.

French monarch's upkeep with an equally extravagant ransom demand.

Most aristocrats who were imprisoned were usually accorded relative freedom of movement, housed in well-appointed rooms with sufficient furniture, a well-stocked larder and wardrobe, servants and were even accompanied by members of their family. Most of this would be at the prisoner's expense. They would also normally be expected to pay for their 'diet and charges' themselves. If someone had been accused of the most serious crime of treason, his property was confiscated by the state and the expense of accommodating him in prison was maintained from the proceeds. A record from the Privy Council proceedings of 1541 records a long list of clothes commissioned from the King's tailor for Arthur Plantagenet, Viscount Lisle, who had been imprisoned in the Tower for his alleged involvement in a plot against Henry VIII (1509–47). The list included a large damask gown, two satin doublets, a velvet and satin nightcap, six pairs of shoes and one pair of slippers. Every prisoner was entitled to an allowance for food, fuel and candles according to a fixed scale that varied in relation to their rank. Prisoners could also get access to medical care, a barber and, by the 18th century, were even allowed visits from their solicitor to prepare for trial.

As the Tower expanded in the 13th and 14th centuries so too did its capacity for housing state prisoners. Each of the newer towers that punctuate the inner and outer curtain walls of the fortress has at one time or another functioned as prison chambers. It is perhaps difficult to imagine any degree of comfort within the bare stone walls that survive today, but the reality in the late medieval and Tudor period was quite different, and the survival of mighty fireplaces and painted interiors gives a glimpse into the everyday surroundings of a well-connected prisoner. These towers were after all used at other

times for other purposes, providing offices for the Royal Household and accommodation for *invited* guests.

Contrary to legend, there was no simple dungeon or large prison block full to the brim with manacled inmates. A list of 1641 that still survives records the following towers being used as prison lodgings: Cradle, Salt, Broad Arrow, Constable, Martin, Well, Beauchamp, Bell, Bloody, Coldharbour and Lanthorn. All of these could house prisoners in some degree of comfort or could be divided up into smaller chambers. Even the Bloody Tower, mythically associated with the murder of the 'Princes in the Tower' in the 15th century, was not the gruesome cell of popular imagination that the name might suggest. Previously known as the Garden Tower (overlooking the Lieutenant of the Tower's garden) it more commonly housed wealthy prisoners like Sir Walter Ralegh in suites of rooms that were well furnished and relatively spacious.

The most important prisoners of all were housed in areas of the Tower where access could be most completely controlled. During the tumultuous years of the 15th and 16th centuries when regime change and the Reformation created an atmosphere of insecurity and suspicion, this meant the rooms of the royal palace or the Lieutenant's lodgings. The range of rooms and chambers that once made up

The Bloody Tower displayed as it may have looked during Sir Walter Ralegh's imprisonment from 1603 to 1616. The interior of the tower was partitioned to provide more living space for Ralegh's family and their servants.

A satirical cartoon depicting Sir Francis Burdett (1770–1844) imprisoned in the Tower Menagerie. Burdett was briefly held at the Tower in 1810 for denouncing flogging in the army and corruption in Parliament.

the royal palace complex to the south of the White Tower frequently accommodated unwilling guests. Anne Boleyn would have stayed here – both before her coronation in 1533 and before her execution just three years later. In 1554, Anne's daughter, Princess Elizabeth, also arrived at the Tower. She too was kept in a suite of four rooms, in the royal palace, with access to servants and the outdoor spaces within the Tower. Unlike her mother, Elizabeth survived her imprisonment and would return to the Tower on the eve of her coronation in 1558.

Other prisoners were not so 'fortunate' with their accommodation and were squeezed in wherever there was space. Particularly during periods of mass arrest, there are records of prisoners in stables, converted corridors and offices and, in 1279, 'a certain woman in the elephant-house' (a building provided in the 1250s for Henry III's elephant in the Royal Menagerie). For the unluckiest of all, 'close imprisonment' meant solitary confine-

ment, usually with access to only the basic necessities and food. Popular locations for this type of incarceration were Tower cellars or storerooms, with earth floors, little light and rats for company. These are the dungeons of popular imagination. Time spent in such inhospitable cells was, however, frequently brief and often used as an interrogation tactic. Faced with the loneliness and fear of a life spent in dark isolation, often with the very real threat of torture, prisoners could be persuaded to confess to their crimes or implicate others. Even the discomfort of day after day spent in a cold damp Tower cellar with no natural light and no bed and no visitors could work just as well. This is the kind of mental torture still familiar to us today, and still used in many parts of the world. It is also perhaps the most enduring image of Tower imprisonment. The words of prisoners who were forced to suffer such hardship survive in diaries, autobiographies and the desperate letters of condemned men.

John Danyell was one, arrested in 1555 accused of involvement in a plan to rob the Exchequer. He was placed in close confinement for a while, explicitly to persuade him to confess and admit his guilt. His statement of April the following year protests:

> I beseech your honours, be good to me. I am a sick man here in a dungeon where I do my ordure and make water and [vomit] in the place I lie in. If I lie here all this night I think I shall not be alive tomorrow... I have no light all day to see my hands perfectly. For God's sake rid me of this dungeon, for I lie sore pained with the stone, among newts and spiders. I do all things in the place that I lie in. I never consented to do evil.

His interrogator's report coldly records the effect the imprisonment had on Danyell a couple of days later: 'Danyell, being yesterday removed to a worse lodging, begins this day to be more open, whereby we perceive he knows all, and trust he will utter the same.'

Many prisoners were allowed access to the kind of diversions that allowed them to pass the time with at least a semblance of equanimity. This was all the more difficult as most had no idea how long they were to be locked up. This was perhaps the greatest torture of all, as hope gradually slipped away with no sign of reprieve or even, in some cases, a trial. Some prisoners found quite creative ways to pass the time. Many committed themselves to lengthy works of literature. Volumes of poetry, of political philosophy and ambitious histories were composed by the more literary-minded of the Tower's inmates. Access to pen, paper

The notebook of Lewis Caerleon (detail), with tables for solar and lunar eclipses, recorded whilst Caerleon was imprisoned in the Tower of London.

and ink was one of the most cherished rights (and one which the Tower authorities repeatedly revoked in order to punish particular prisoners).

Lewis Caerleon spent the year of 1485 drawing complex tables for solar and lunar eclipses from observations he took as a prisoner. Caerleon was a physican to the deposed royal family of Edward V and to Margaret Beaufort, Countess of Richmond and mother of Henry Tudor. Richard III (1483–5) arrested him on suspicion of disloyalty during the anxious and uncertain years of his reign, before Henry Tudor's triumph later in the year (when Caerleon was released). The physician's notebook pointedly remarks that he is making new tables to replace those stolen by Richard III after his arrest.

One of the most distinguished polymaths to occupy the Tower was Henry Percy, 9th Earl of Northumberland, arrested on suspicion of complicity in the Gunpowder Plot of 1605. Known by the nickname of the 'Wizard Earl', Percy was a scientist with a special interest in astrology and alchemy. He was imprisoned between 1606 and 1621 in the Martin Tower but was provided with scientific instruments, a study, library, a great chamber, a drawing room, two dining rooms and accommodation for his servants. His son was lodged next door in the Brick Tower, with a personal tutor. Guests flocked to dinner provided by a well-stocked kitchen that continued to offer the luxury and variety of delicacies that Percy had enjoyed on the outside. The Earl was also allowed to build a still-house

to conduct experiments.

Sir Walter Ralegh spent enough time at the Tower to combine both literary and scientific pursuits. He conducted experiments in his own still house in the Tower gardens (where he also played bowls with fellow scientist, Henry Percy) whilst embarking on a *History of the World* using his Tower library of over 500 books.

Treason and traitors

R alegh was not an unusual Tower prisoner. His long-drawn out death sentence (finally carried out 15 years after it was originally passed) was for allegedly plotting against the accession of James I (1603–25). His guilt was difficult to prove, but in times of national insecurity, accusations of treason were usually all that was required to justify prolonged periods of imprisonment, with or without trial, and even execution. Many of those accused of treason were guilty of nothing more than ending up on the losing side of one of England's bitter and complex dynastic wars. When power lay exclusively within the upper ranks of society, it was virtually impossible to be a nobleman without committing to one particular side or another. The spoils of victory were plentiful; the risks of defeat manifest.

Henry Percy, 9th Earl of Northumberland (1564–1632) spent 15 years in the Tower on suspicion of being involved in the Gunpowder Plot. This painting by JMW Turner, c1831, shows Percy's daughters visiting him after his release.

Richard II arriving at the Tower of London in 1399 (painted c1460–80) after his fall from power.

Richard II (1377–99) fell from power in 1399 and was briefly held at the Tower before being moved to a less public confinement (and less obvious death) in Pontefract Castle. He was not the first, and certainly not the last, to be taken to the Tower as a statement of political subjugation. King Richard, 'the highest man in England now the lowest of the low' (as the poet John Gower described him), was placed explicitly and publicly under the

control of the new power in the land, his cousin Henry Bolingbroke, Duke of Lancaster, soon to have himself crowned as Henry IV (1399–1413).

Bolingbroke's grandson, Henry VI (1422–61 and 1470–1), the last Lancastrian king, died at the Tower in 1471. His fortunes, and that of his rival to the throne, Edward IV (1461–70 and 1471–83), had waxed and waned during the dynastic struggle of the previous decade known as the Wars of the Roses. His final imprisonment ended with his death in the Wakefield Tower. (Tradition has long claimed that he was murdered.) Only a dozen years later, on the death of Edward IV, the Tower became home, prison and resting place for his sons, the young 'Princes in the Tower', Edward V and Richard, Duke of York. Controversy still rages over how and by whose hand the princes died. Tudor accounts placed responsibility firmly at the door of their uncle and protector Richard of Gloucester, who had himself crowned in 1483 as Richard III. Yet the Tudors were themselves prejudiced by their own desire to discredit the regime that *they* replaced at the Battle of Bosworth in 1485.

The cold reality was that the imprison-

Robert Devereux, 2nd Earl of Essex (1566–1601), in a miniature attributed to Nicholas Hilliard. Essex was deprived of his office of Lord Lieutenant of Ireland in 1600, after concluding an unfavourable truce with Irish rebels. The following year, after an unsuccessful revolt against Elizabeth I, he was captured and beheaded at the Tower.

ment (and occasional murder) of political rivals was not uncommon, although also not without controversy. Murder behind the silent walls of a fortress could indeed be more straightforward than killing an opponent on the battlefield. The Tower was still a royal palace: access was difficult and witnesses rare. Even so, other fortresses could be even more remote and better suited to secret executions. The events surrounding the death of Edward II (1307–27) at Berkeley Castle and Richard II (1377–99) at Pontefract are still uncertain.

Each change in the political landscape brought new prisoners to the Tower, as the new power in the land incarcerated the supporters of the previous reign and, in extreme cases, made them disappear. Attempting to predict change and make preparations accordingly could also be dangerous. The Tower was often the home for those who had failed to change sides at the right moment. In the last years of the reign of Elizabeth I (1558–1603), there was a queue of prisoners who had tried to second guess who Elizabeth would name as her successor. The Lieutenant of the Tower himself, Sir Michael Blount, found himself briefly a prisoner, for making arrangements to secure the Tower (and his office) on the event of the Queen's death. The Earl of Essex went to the Tower and his execution in 1601 for completely running out of patience with the old Queen and leading a rebellion. The uncertainty and instability continued after Elizabeth's death. The 17th century saw the Tower accommodate in turn royalist supporters of Charles I (1625–49) and, a little over a decade later,

Henry VI
(1421–71)

PRISONER: 1465–70 AND 1471

Henry VI (1422–61 and 1470–1) was the last Lancastrian king of England and one of two English kings to die at the Tower (the other was the uncrowned Edward V).

Henry acceded to the throne before his first birthday, after the premature death of his admired father, Henry V, victor of Agincourt and celebrated war hero. In 1437, his mother, Catherine of Valois, died and Henry came of age. His reign was one of great political instability culminating in the dynastic conflict known as the Wars of the Roses when two branches of the royal house of Plantagenet, the houses of Lancaster and York, fought for the throne.

A combination of Henry's military weakness and the political ambition of Richard, Duke of York (who had been assumed heir to the throne until the birth of Henry's own son), lost Henry the throne in 1461. For the next five years he lived as an exile in Scotland and the north of England, sheltered by supporters, but was betrayed into the hands of his royal rival, Edward IV, son of Richard of York, in 1465.

For five years, Henry was held a prisoner at the Tower, whilst his wife, Margaret of Anjou, and his son lived in exile in France. The deposed king was allowed visitors and to attend daily Mass. Edward IV spent large sums of money on retainers to look after Henry and on food and drink. Meanwhile, the battle for a disputed crown continued and in October 1470 Henry suddenly

Henry VI by an unknown artist, c1540. The King died at the Tower in 1471

found himself back on the throne. Richard Neville, Earl of Warwick ('The Kingmaker') had changed sides and arranged a marriage for his own daughter with Henry's son Prince Edward – the Lancastrian heir to the throne.

The restored House of Lancaster lasted only six months. At the decisive battles of Barnet and Tewkesbury in the spring of 1471, Henry's supporters were defeated and Warwick and Prince Edward slain. Henry found himself back in his Tower prison. This time, it seems, Edward IV was prepared to take no chances on a further reversal of fortune. Whether by direct order or not,

Henry died at the Tower within a suspiciously short period of time. Later accounts would claim that he was brutally murdered while at prayer in the Wakefield Tower, but it is also argued that he died of despair and ill health brought on by the death of his son, the arrest of his wife and his irretrievable defeat.

The death of Henry VI at the Tower is still commemorated by the annual Ceremony of Lilies and Roses. Tributes are laid at the spot of his alleged murder by representatives of King's College, Cambridge and Eton school, two educational establishments founded by the King.

those responsible for his death. There was no simple right or wrong. Guilt depended on politics and regime change.

Of course, there were genuine causes of concern. The Tudor dynasty's claim to power was notoriously weak, and its consistent inability to secure its own survival by producing a male heir made it open to plots led by members of the old Plantagenet royal family, or alternative rulers within its own family. Bringing the Reformation to England did not help stability. Henry VIII's establishment of the Church of England and complete rejection of papal supremacy was motivated by his need to obtain a divorce from Catherine of Aragon. In attempting to remarry and produce a son, he sought to consolidate the Tudor dynasty for the next generation. Instead, he created half a century of religious confusion and political instability that brought many more prisoners to the Tower.

Thomas More and John Fisher were but the first of those who found they could not accept the direction that the country was heading and so were labelled traitors and condemned to death. More, who had previously been Henry VIII's Chancellor, was taken to the Tower in 1534 for refusing to accept that Henry could place himself at the head of an 'Anglican' Church and deny papal supremacy. At first, like many prisoners of his status, his confinement was not unduly harsh, as Henry sought to persuade him to change his mind. Eventually, he was accused of treason, and denied access to visitors, books and writing materials. His wife Alice (who paid 15 shillings a week for his board and lodgings) despaired:

I marvel that you should lie in that close and filthy prison, shut up among mice and rats, when you might be abroad at your liberty, with the favour and goodwill of the King and his Council. And seeing you have in Chelsea a right fair house, your library, gallery, orchard, where you might in the company of me, your children, and household be merry, I muse what you mean here thus fondly to tarry.

Her appeal was to no avail. More 'had become a monk at last' (as the historian Peter Ackroyd has suggested) and dedicated himself to contemplation and writing (when he was allowed the means so to do). He composed both his *Dialogue of Comfort against Tribulation* and *Treatise upon the Passion* as a Tower prisoner. He was executed in 1535.

In the next few decades, being Protestant or Catholic became not only a statement of conscience but also frequently a declaration of political allegiance. Rebellions and conspiracies did happen and the consequences for those who were defeated and captured could well prove fatal. Those found guilty of treason were usually executed, many facing the traditional end of traitors: to be hanged, cut down whilst still alive, disembowelled and quartered. Before their execution, however, they were often still imprisoned according to their status in life. Nobles were even accorded a noble death – the quick and merciful release of beheading, rather than the brutal and messy execution by hanging, drawing and quartering.

There were plots to replace Mary I (1553–8) with Princess Elizabeth and plots

Anne Boleyn
(c1500–36)

PRISONER: 1536

Anne Boleyn in the Tower by Edouard Cibot, 1835. Henry VIII's second wife was executed on Tower Green in 1536.

Henry VIII married his second wife, Anne Boleyn, in January 1533. In advance of Anne's coronation on 1 June, the King and Queen stayed at the Tower of London where the royal apartments had been refurbished and other lodgings rebuilt or erected for the joyous occasion. However, just three years later, Anne was tried and executed within the walls of the Tower.

Anne proved unable to provide Henry with the son he so desperately sought and by the end of 1535 he was anxious to marry again. On 2 May 1536, Anne was arrested at Greenwich. She was accused of adultery with four men and incest with her own brother, George Boleyn, Viscount Rochford. In committing these crimes, she was also accused of plotting the King's death and indirectly damaging his health when news of her adultery was made known to him. On her arrival at the Tower, Anne is reported to have asked, 'Shall I go into a dungeon?' 'No madam', came the reply, 'You shall go into the lodging you lay in at your coronation'.

Anne was tried in the Lieutenant's lodgings on the site of today's Queen's House (rebuilt just after the event in 1540). Her judge was her own uncle, Thomas Howard, Duke of Norfolk. Anne always denied the charges against her and the evidence was circumstantial to say the least. Nonetheless, guilty verdicts were passed. Her brother and the other four men were executed on Tower Hill on 17 May.

Anne's behaviour in her own lodg-ings as she saw all hope fade, became increasingly hysterical. Letters sent by the Constable of the Tower, Sir William Kingston, to Henry's chief minister, Thomas Cromwell, record that she would kneel down and weep and 'in the same sorrow' fall 'into a great laughing'. By the day of her execution, 19 May 1536, Anne had regained her composure. A letter from Kingston describes how he found the Queen that morning: 'She said "I heard say the executioner was very good, and I have a little neck", and then put her hands about it, laughing heartily. I have seen many men and also women executed, and that they have been in great sorrow, and to my knowledge this lady has much joy in death'. On the scaffold, Anne accepted her fate with equanimity: 'I am come hither to accuse no man, nor to speak anything of that, whereof I am accused and con-demned to die, but I pray God save the King and send him long to reign over you, for a gentler nor a more merciful prince was there never. and to me he was ever a good and sovereign lord.'

The Queen was granted special dispensation to be beheaded with a sword. An expert French executioner had been brought in, who carried out his task quickly and effectively. The prayer book that Anne is said to have taken with her to the scaffold, survives at Hever Castle. In it, Anne wrote, 'Remember me when you do pray, that hope doth lead from day to day'. The Queen was buried in the Chapel Royal of St Peter ad Vincula, close by the scaffold site on Tower Green.

This inscription was carved into the walls of the Beauchamp Tower by Philip Howard, Earl of Arundel (1557–95) during his imprisonment. Arundel died in the Beauchamp Tower after ten years in prison; he was canonised in 1970.

William Penn (1644–1718) wrote the first version of his great masterpiece, No Cross, No Crown, *whilst a prisoner in the Tower of London in 1668.*

to replace Elizabeth I (1558–1603) with practically any suitable Catholic alternative. Both queens could be justifiably anxious and suspicious. Yet in such a climate of fear, virtually everyone who was not (respectively) a Catholic or a Protestant was guilty by association. Both queens could be spectacularly ruthless. Opposition to the established religion was still considered heresy and in itself punishable by death. Most of those so accused were not considered worthy of imprisonment at the Tower and were burned alive at Smithfield or elsewhere. The Tower remained the home for the most important heretics and the leaders of alleged conspiracies.

Philip Howard, Earl of Arundel, converted to Catholicism in 1584 and was imprisoned by Elizabeth I at the Tower for ten years. By becoming the leading Catholic peer in the country, he was automatically perceived as a threat to national security, especially given England's hostilities with Catholic Spain. He was sentenced to death in 1589 and lived under the daily expectation of execution, but eventually died of illness, still a captive at the Tower. Howard was joined by others lower down the social order. Under Elizabeth I, it was illegal simply to be a Roman Catholic priest in England; many were arrested and charged with treason, whether they were caught administering the sacraments or not. They were considered by definition enemies of the state. Some were released into exile, whilst others died traitors' deaths. Many were tortured, to implicate others (or themselves) in conspiracies against the life of the Queen.

Being imprisoned on the basis of religious faith was not a new thing. Indeed, the ugly tradition of religious intolerance in England stretched back many centuries. In 1240 new taxes on England's Jewish population led to mass detentions at the Tower for those who were unable to pay. In 1278, six hundred Jews were imprisoned until the following year on charges of 'clipping' the coinage. Prisoners of religious conscience did not disappear after the 16th century either. In 1668, William Penn, the Quaker (and later the founder of Pennsylvania), was locked away for publishing an attack on the Athanasian doctrine of the Trinity and theory of Justification that formed part of the later 17th-century Anglican Church theology. He was offered release if he recanted. Penn declared, 'The Tower is to me the worst argument in the world. My prison shall be my grave before I shall budge a jot'. He was, however, released the following year.

William Davidson (1781–1820), a 'Cato Street Conspirator', one of the few known black prisoners of the Tower. He was hanged on 1 May 1820 at Newgate gaol.

Such prisoners of religious conscience have been joined over the centuries by those whose political beliefs were considered treacherous or dangerous by the state. Once again, this group includes both those who took active parts in very real conspiracies against the monarchy or government, and those whose outspoken radicalism by itself defined them as traitors. The most famous are perhaps the Gunpowder Plot conspirators of 1605 who were found guilty of plotting to blow up the royal family and the aristocracy at the opening of Parliament. William FitzOsbert was imprisoned in the Tower in 1196 for 'seditiously moving the common people to seek liberty' (or, more prosaically, protesting against taxation). As late as the early 19th century, the radical reformers known as the Cato Street Conspirators were detained and later executed for plotting to blow up the Cabinet and proclaiming a provisional government.

Peter Wentworth MP was imprisoned in the Tower on four separate occasions in the later 16th century for his obstinate belief in the right of parliament to debate whatever it thought important. This included religious issues and the thorny question of who Elizabeth I ought to choose as her successor. In the 18th century, individual opponents of the government were locked up for making a stand for political reform. John Wilkes MP, champion of a free press (or dangerous demagogue, depending on your point of view at the time), went to the Tower in 1763 after criticising George III (1760–1820) in print. Wilkes transformed his prosecution into a campaign for people's rights against oppression; he was released after a few days and later became Lord Mayor of London. In 1771, the Lord Mayor of the day was himself imprisoned. Brass Crosby was briefly incarcerated in the Tower along with Alderman Richard Oliver for supporting the right of City of London printers to publish parliamentary debates. Whilst individual campaigners often had their own particular ambitions and motivation for making a stand, the 18th century saw a greater demand from an emerging middle class for fairer political representation and participation. Changes to the electoral system were blocked by a ruling oligarchic elite with vested interests in keeping the status quo. The experience of the American War of Independence persuaded the British government that no quarter should be given to political reformers at home.

Yet imprisonment in the Tower was becoming more unpalatable by the decade. It was considered unacceptable for the state to incarcerate people in the Tower simply for speaking out against injustice or for following political conscience. Tower imprisonment was a very public affair. The very strength of its image as a symbol of state power now became its weakness. Oliver and Crosby were released after two months of political pressure from their supporters who had paralysed civic government in the capital. Their triumphal procession to Mansion House included 53 carriages and a 21-gun salute.

In 1794, in the aftermath of the French Revolution, the Habeas Corpus Act (which

Lady Jane Grey
(1537–54)

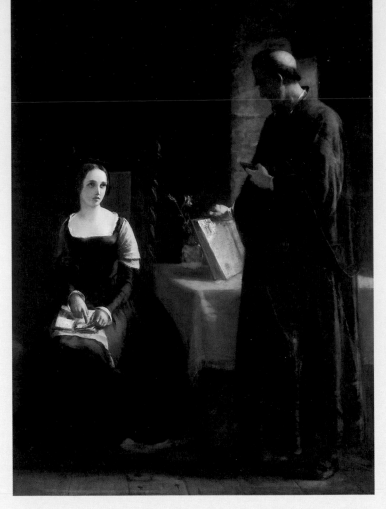

Lady Jane Grey and John de Feckenham, Abbot of Westminster and private chaplain to Mary I. The Queen sent Feckenham to visit Jane in the Tower, two days before her death, to convert her to Romanism. He later became a prisoner of the Tower himself during the reign of Elizabeth I. Painting by James Clarke Hook, RA (1819–1907).

PRISONER: 1553–4

Lady Jane Grey was proclaimed queen in July 1553 and entered the Tower with her new husband in preparation for her coronation procession, in accordance with a tradition begun in the medieval period. She was the grand-daughter of Henry VIII's sister and a Protestant.

Jane had been married to Lord Guildford Dudley in an attempt to subvert the Tudor line of succession away from Edward VI's half-sister and rightful heir, the devoutly Roman Catholic Mary Tudor, to the Protestant Grey family. As the daughter-in-law of the powerful John Dudley, Duke of Northumberland, it was anticipated that Jane would prove a malleable sovereign. The Duke had developed a taste for power during the reign of the young Edward VI when he served as Lord Protector.

The Dudley bid for the throne through Queen Jane had every appearance of succeeding, as all the major politicians of the day supported the plan. However, the weight of popular feeling for Princess Mary had not been taken into account and the tide soon began to turn. Northumberland was arrested by his former allies while on his way to capture Princess Mary in Norfolk in July 1553. Mary was proclaimed queen soon after.

Jane was now a prisoner at the Tower. It is not known exactly where she was confined, but 'The Chronicle of Queen Jane, and of Two Years of Queen Mary', by an unknown officer of the Tower, c1554, records her dining 'at Partridge's House', which has often been interpreted as No. 5 Tower Green. Another popular theory was that Jane was incarcerated in the Beauchamp Tower, because of the 'IANE' inscriptions that survive in the upper chamber. It is not known whether Jane and her husband were imprisoned together.

The former queen and Lord Guildford were tried and condemned as traitors at the Guildhall in November 1553. Queen Mary was merciful and granted a reprieve from the death sentence, allowing the couple to remain prisoners of the Tower. They were granted a degree of liberty and allowed access to the Tower gardens. However, the Protestant Wyatt Rebellion, quashed in 1554, made Jane's existence more of a threat to the Catholic monarch and the involvement of Jane's father in the rebellion sealed her fate.

Queen Mary ordered her clemency revoked unless the couple converted to the Catholic faith. Both refused and were condemned to death. Lord Guildford Dudley was executed on Tower Hill at 10 o'clock on 12 February 1554. The 'Chronicle' states that Jane saw him being led to execution, and his decapitated corpse afterwards. Jane was taken to her own execution an hour after her husband. She said a prayer, forgave her executioner and was led to the block blindfolded. One of the privileged few, Jane was beheaded within the Tower walls, on a scaffold erected next to the White Tower.

had been made law in 1679 and placed limitations on the state from holding prisoners without trial) was suspended. Members of the London Corresponding Society who argued for constitutional reform were arrested and accused of high treason; they were held without trial for six months in the Tower but most charges were eventually dropped. Even when imprisonment followed a more obvious case of rebellion, there was a growing discomfort at the benefits of Tower imprisonment. Concerns grew as the condemned used the platform of their execution scaffold for political proclamations. The Jacobite rebel Lord Balmerino used this stage in 1746 to accuse the British of atrocities:

> I have heard since I came to this place that there has been a most wicked report spread and mentioned in several of the newspapers, that His Royal Highness, the Prince [Bonnie Prince Charlie, the Young Pretender] before the Battle of Culloden, had given out orders that no quarters should be given to the enemy. This is such an unchristian thing and so unlike that gallant Prince that nobody that knows him will believe it... I am convinced that it is a malicious report industriously spread to excuse themselves for the murders they were guilty of in calm blood after the battle.

The last beheading took place on Tower Hill in 1747 and the last public executions on that site were in 1780. The Cato Street Conspirators of 1820 were the last prisoners of the Tower for almost a hundred years. By this point, the Tower was becoming an increasingly popular visitor attrac-

Simon Fraser, 11th Lord Lovat (1667?–1747), became the last person to be beheaded on Tower Hill, at the age of 80, for his support of the Jacobite uprisings against George II. This engraving by Samuel Ireland, published in 1747, is entitled 'Lovat's Ghost on Pilgrimage'.

tion and its continued role as a state prison sat uncomfortably alongside its new displays of Spanish torture instruments and Anne Boleyn's axe.

Yet even in more recent decades the Tower continued to live up to its grim reputation. During the Second World War, the Tower operated briefly as a collection centre for German prisoners of war. In 1939, crews of submariners and captured pilots were held, usually for only a few days, before transfer to permanent camps in the north of England. In 1941, Rudolf Hess, Hitler's Deputy Reichsführer, was brought to the Tower after his mysterious flight to Scotland, apparently to open negotiations for peace. The Tower, it seems, remained the most obvious place to bring such an important state prisoner, even in the middle of the 20th century. Hess was lodged in the King's House (now the Queen's House) but left within a week for a less public detention in a Victorian country house in Surrey.

The story of imprisonment at the Tower is not simply a historical curiosity. It is of course far less acceptable to execute political rivals today than in previous eras. However, in times of national insecurity, cherished rights and freedoms continue to become singularly elusive, as governments evoke emergency measures to crack down on opposition. Methods of mental and physical torture used over the centuries are still used around the world today. Food and sleep deprivation, refusal of access to natural light and being forced to stand for long periods in contorted positions were all employed by Tower authorities keen to extract information

or confessions. According to Amnesty International, these methods still form part of the techniques of what is known as 'interrogation in depth'. The Tower of London stands as testament to long traditions of political imprisonment and of state power.

The guards

Rudolf Hess left a permanent reminder of his stay at the Tower in the form of a signed sheet of Tower notepaper presented to one of his guards. The relationship of prisoner and guard has been of particular importance to both throughout the Tower's history. From the early 1300s, the Tower has been guarded by between thirty and forty armed footmen paid to keep undesirables outside and prisoners inside. In the Tudor period, the guards were issued with uniforms similar to the Yeomen of the Guard (the royal bodyguard) and became established as Yeoman Warders. They were (and continue to be) led by a Chief Yeoman Warder (or Porter) and a Yeoman (or Gentleman) Gaoler. The latter, as the name suggests, had specific responsibility for prisoners.

Portrait of a Yeoman Warder, 1746, by George Beare. This is the earliest known portrait of one of the Tower's guards.

Shackled prisoners await their turn in the dock in a 15th-century representation of the court of King's Bench. Yeoman Warders escorted their prisoners to trial with the Yeoman Gaoler. The Gaoler's ceremonial axe would be turned towards the prisoner on the return journey if a sentence of death had been passed.

Many prisoners were accommodated in the Yeoman Warders' own lodgings, paying fees to their guard for room and board. The warders were personally responsible for the security of their charges and would be disciplined for negligence. Colonel Adam Williamson, Deputy Lieutenant of the Tower from 1722, advised his warders:

There is no faith to be given to prisoners, and I advise all officers to do their duty with regularity, as well as civility, and to keep to the letter of the orders without relaxing, for if you deviate a little from them, they are never satisfied till you give more and more liberties, till at last, you must either become criminal or in ceasing to gratify them, they fall out with you, revile and treat you as an ill-natured man and tyrannical in your office.

For close prisoners, warders were instructed to stay with the prisoner day and night, to allow them no visitors, and usually no pen, ink or paper. Any delivery of fresh clothes was to be examined and the room searched daily. All food was to be similarly searched (including the 'opening of pies'). In 1722 no wine was

to be admitted to any close prisoner, in flasks, unless the covering of the flask be first taken off, and that bottle looked through by holding a lighted candle behind it, and all empty bottles as well as full to be examined the same way, and that, always by the Gentleman Gaoler, and no liquor likewise to be admitted in stone bottles, but the liquor first to be poured out and the bottles very carefully examined.

For the prisoner, getting on well with his personal warder could nonetheless mean access to additional luxuries and comforts. Henry Laurens, US Minister to Holland (and earlier President of the Continental Congress) was captured during the American War of Independence and sent to the Tower. During his 15 months at the fortress in 1780 and 1781, he built up a close friendship with his warder, James Futerell. The warder and his family made attempts to make his time at the Tower more agreeable. They remained friends even after Laurens's eventual release and return to the United States. But such close relationships could be abused. Many of the accounts of successful escape attempts from the Tower have involved the complicity (willingly or unwittingly) on the part of a warder who

had become too relaxed in the company of his charge.

The very first recorded prisoner of the Tower also in fact became the first successful escapee. In 1101, Ranulf Flambard hosted a grand feast and was particularly generous with the wine. Once his guards were intoxicated, he used a rope (smuggled inside one of the wine barrels) to climb down from the upper chambers of the White Tower and escape. In 1322, Lord Roger Mortimer of Wigmore arrived at the Tower after his involvement in a failed insurrection against Edward II (1307–27). The following summer, in the dead of night, Mortimer succeeded in drugging his guards by some form of noxious drink and broke out through the wall of his chamber. In 1534, Alice Tankerville persuaded one of the Lieutenant of the Tower's servants, John Bawde, to help her escape. Bawde purchased two ropes and copied the key to the outer door of the prison chambers. The inner door was fastened with a bone pin, which the two conspirators managed to work loose. One night, Alice escaped to the roof of St Thomas's Tower and there met with Bawde. Together, they slid down

Gruffudd ap Llywelyn, Prince of Wales, attempted to escape from the White Tower in 1244. He tied together sheets, but they unravelled during his descent and he broke his neck in the fall. This illustration is from Matthew Paris's 13th-century chronicle, Historia Anglorum

In 1716, Winifred Maxwell engineered the escape of her husband, William, Earl of Nithsdale (1676–1744), by disguising him as one of her friends. She even remained in his cell for some time afterward, keeping up a pretend conversation until she judged that her husband had got well clear of the Tower. Painting by Emily Mary Osborn (1834–93).

their ropes on to the wharf and into a boat that they navigated until they were clear of the Tower precincts. Landing outside the Tower walls, they made their way up Tower Hill but were apprehended by the watch, one of whom recognised Alice. There was no happy ending to this escape. Alice and her accomplice were executed.

The security of the prisoners was the ultimate responsibility of the Constable of the Tower, although from the later Tudor period onwards, the chief resident Tower official was more frequently the Constable's deputy, the Lieutenant. Constables and Lieutenants had frequently to pay for the diet and expense of lodging for the prisoners themselves, and claimed back their costs from the Exchequer. This was a system that could be open to abuse, although there were other means to enrichment through various tolls and the power of political patronage. In general, however, their success and longevity in their post was in part due to their ability

to ensure a tight administration and not to allow anyone to escape. Some earned quite unattractive reputations as a result.

Sir William Waad, the Lieutenant of the Tower who oversaw much of Ralegh's imprisonment and the interrogation of Guy Fawkes, was known as 'that beast Waad' by the former. He was succeeded by Sir Gervase Elwes who ended up hanged in chains on Tower Hill for colluding in the murder of a prisoner, Sir Thomas Overbury, in 1613. Waad may have been particularly unfairly maligned because of his actions in curtailing the lax discipline of his predecessor. It seems that those prisoners who were allowed the liberty of the Tower had been generally allowed to entertain all manner of visitors and servants. Waad had to re-institute regulations that, for example, removed Lady Ralegh from lodging with her husband at the Tower to her house outside the walls on Tower Hill. This was not the only occasion where such measures became necessary. In 1686, regulations were again re-issued as relaxed security had allowed 'a great concourse of people' wandering about the Tower, 'a thing most dangerous in respect of the small guard allowed for the keeping of a place of such consequence'.

The Constable (or the Lieutenant) also exercised the right of direct access to the sovereign, and in at least one case intervened to appeal against the harsh treatment of a prisoner under interrogation. Anne Askew, the only woman known to have been tortured at the Tower, was racked in 1546 in an attempt to implicate other Protestants at court, including

Princess Elizabeth (1533–1603)

Princess Elizabeth, by an unknown artist, c1546. The Princess was granted spacious accommodation and was allowed to walk in the gardens and gallery of the royal palace during her imprisonment.

PRISONER: 1554

Elizabeth I's (1558–1603) reign as queen of England was so long and so successful that it is difficult to remember there was a time when her execution seemed more likely than her coronation. The young Princess Elizabeth was one of the Tower's most famous inmates. She was imprisoned by her half-sister Mary I in the dangerous days when the Catholic queen lived in fear of Protestant insurrection. Mary suspected that Elizabeth was involved in a plot against her, led by the traitor Sir Thomas Wyatt.

Elizabeth was committed to the Tower on 17 March 1554. On hearing the news, she wrote a harrowing letter to Mary, reminding her that she had promised not to condemn her without proof. She hoped that 'evil persuasions' would 'persuade not one sister against the other', and filled up the blank page with scribbles to prevent anyone else from inserting extra text as a deception. However, Mary was relentless. 'Oh Lord!' said Elizabeth, as she entered the Tower, 'I never thought to have come here as a prisoner'.

Had Elizabeth committed treason? She had indeed acted suspiciously, keeping away from court on grounds of ill health. Wyatt and the rebels had tried to involve Elizabeth in their affairs but, as she protested, this did not mean she was guilty. Even if she secretly wished for the plot to succeed, she was far too clever to commit herself in writing.

Elizabeth reached the Tower by boat. One account describes how she arrived at Traitors' Gate but this was probably a dramatic embellishment because it is known that she walked over a draw bridge, rather than arriving through a watergate. A huge number of guards were drawn up to receive her. Elizabeth, successfully making a play for their sympathy, said that it 'needed not for me, being, alas, but a weak woman'. Some of the guards are supposed to have taken off their caps, knelt down, and called out 'God save your grace!' as Elizabeth passed under the Bloody Tower. Even the Lord Treasurer and the Earl of Sussex were deeply troubled and wept as they locked the doors on the Queen's half-sister.

Elizabeth's imprisonment was comfortable enough physically but a psychological strain. She had four rooms in the old palace. But Elizabeth was now in the same building where her mother, Anne Boleyn, had been imprisoned before her trial and execution, and the scaffold used to execute Lady Jane Grey still stood outside. Elizabeth could only wait and hope as the case against the conspirators progressed. Their leader, Wyatt, was eventually executed on 11 April 1554 and it soon became clear that there was not enough evidence to convict Elizabeth. Soon after, she was allowed to leave the Tower in order to endure a more comfortable form of house arrest in the country.

In 1559 Elizabeth returned to the Tower under very different circumstances. On 14 January, after the traditional celebrations, she left the fortress to ride through the City of London to her coronation at Westminster Abbey.

Queen Catherine Parr. The torture was apparently carried out by the Lord Chancellor, Lord Wriothesley, and his aide, Sir Richard Rich. The Lieutenant, Thomas Knyvett, appealed to the King to end her inhumane treatment. He was partly successful. Askew was executed at Smithfield.

Execution or survival

Askew, like most who suffered similar fates, was given a public execution at one of the various sites across the capital provided for this purpose. Public executions were customarily popular. For the execution of the Jacobite rebel lords on Tower Hill in 1746, special stands were erected and street sellers hawked snacks and 'last confessions'. Private executions within the walls of the Tower were only granted on seven occasions, during the Tudor era. Henry VIII's queens, Anne Boleyn and Catherine Howard (along with her lady-in-waiting, Viscountess Rochford), and Lady Jane Grey who tried to seize the throne in 1553 were allowed such a privilege on account of their status. Before this, William, Lord Hastings had been summarily executed near Tower Green in 1483, apparently on the orders of Richard of Gloucester as he engineered his seizure of the throne. In this case, there was extremely questionable legality for a dangerous public execution.

This was also the case in 1541. Margaret Pole, Countess of Salisbury, had been arrested in 1538 on suspicion of conspiracy against the ageing and increasingly paranoid Henry VIII. Her son, Cardinal Reginald Pole, was certainly active on the Continent, campaigning for a Catholic invasion of England, but it is extremely unlikely that the 70-year-old Countess posed any real threat. Her real crime was to be the head of a large and fertile family of alternative claimants to the English throne. A blundering executioner 'hacked her head and shoulders to pieces'. The last of the seven, the popular Robert Devereux, Earl of Essex, was also executed away from the public gaze in 1601 'lest the acclamation of the people might have been a temptation unto him' to denounce his fate and his Queen from the scaffold. The state made detailed precautions to ensure his execution went ahead smoothly. Two axe men were hired, 'because if one faints, the other may perform it'. They arrived secretly and the tool of their trade was brought into the fortress separately.

These seven Tudor beheadings are not, however, the only executions to have taken place within the Tower's walls. In 1743, Farquhar Shaw and the cousins Samuel and Malcolm Macpherson, three of the so-called Black Watch 'Mutineers', were shot at dawn on Tower Green in front of the rest of their regiment. The Black

The Beheading of the Rebel Lords on Great Tower Hill, 1746. Tower Hill was the principal place of execution for Tower prisoners found guilty of treason. Some 125 people are known to have died there, most by beheading.

Watch had been established to police or 'watch' the Highlands of Scotland during the Jacobite troubles. They were constituted from loyal Scottish soldiers (many from relatively wealthy Scottish families) who had agreed to this specific commission on behalf of the English government. In 1743, however, they were ordered to London, ostensibly to be inspected by the king. Rumours circulated that they were instead to be sent abroad and, viewing this as a completely unacceptable abuse of their commission, over a hundred soldiers turned around on their march south to return home. They were soon rounded up, taken under arrest to the Tower and three of the alleged ringleaders were shot.

During the First World War 11 spies of various nationalities were executed at the Tower by firing squad. Later still, in 1941, Josef Jakobs, a sergeant of the German Meteorological Service, was also executed as a spy in the Rifle Range. This was the last execution to take place within the walls of the fortress. There is no monument to these latter-day victims of Tower justice but they are as much a part of the story of Tower imprisonment as their medieval and Tudor predecessors.

Only a minority of Tower prisoners were actually executed. Some died after languishing in their cells for years. A few managed to escape. The majority were released, banished into exile or transferred to other gaols after interrogation or when they were no longer considered a threat. Their stories are, understandably perhaps, of less immediate impact than the more salacious accounts of executed traitors and unfaithful queens. Yet the gruesome nature of parts of the Tower story has served to obscure the whole picture of imprisonment. Just as the role of the Tower as a state prison has been overstressed over the years and hidden its history as a fortress and a palace, the bloody accounts of torture and violent death have overshadowed the most important element of the imprisonment story.

The Tower stands as a symbol of state power precisely because the state has encouraged it to be so. The clear message over the centuries has been: 'Question the political or religious status quo and you could end up here; we will keep you here for as long as we wish and you will have no access if we so determine to the niceties of normal justice.' Whether or not an individual really did pose a threat to national security, the state had the power to invoke emergency measures which meant that a prisoner could be effectively incarcerated without trial (or a fair one) at the state's pleasure.

The Tower may no longer be used as a state prison, but the story of political imprisonment that it has to tell remains an important and relevant one today.

The East Casemates Rifle Range, c1915, where Josef Jakobs was executed in 1941.

The chair used for the execution of Josef Jakobs in 1941, which has remained in the collection of the Royal Armouries ever since.

MYTH AND IMAGE

Fortress and prison

The idea of the Tower of London as a state prison is one that has long outlasted that particular function. From at least the time of Henry III (1216–72) it had a well-deserved reputation as a prison, albeit a very ad hoc and often inconvenient one. This view is reflected not only in contemporary accounts but also occasionally glimpsed in early English poetry. However, it was not really until the 16th century that the public perception of the Tower as a prison began to be heightened by more widely available cultural influences. With some irony, its enduring image as a place of dingy incarceration and torture, disseminated through art and literature as well as popular publications, coincided with an end to executions and the gradual removal of prisoners from the Tower.

How this somewhat topsy-turvy view of its history came about is not always straightforward: it has chiefly to do with the historical importance of some of the darker events that took place within the Tower, together with its reputation as an intimidating citadel, which the state authorities regularly encouraged.

Three main contributors seem to have helped in creating the myth: the guards of the Tower, who also acted as guides to its visitors (and still do); early literary writers dealing with English history, most significantly William Shakespeare; and writers and artists of the Romantic era. These influences have been opposed at times by the historians of the Tower, who were few and far between before the 19th century.

A Yeoman Warder demonstrates the torture instrument known as Skeffington's Irons to tourists in the Spanish Armoury, taken from a guidebook of c.1820

The Execution of Lady Jane Grey (detail) by Paul Delaroche, 1833. This painting was the hit of the Paris Salon the following year and became one of the most enduring images from the Tower's bloody history.

There is a fascinating interplay between the representatives of these two extremes, which were not nearly so exclusive as the modern visitor or historian would perhaps like to believe. That is of course the nature of a myth – the explanation of a little-understood phenomenon through memorable story telling.

Truth stranger than fiction

Daring escapes from the parapet, regicide and infanticide, the execution of young queens: the true histories behind the spoken, written or drawn images of prisoners of the Tower were often just as dramatic or shrouded in mystery. Records of these events had their origins in state papers and early historical accounts. As an example, the mysterious death in custody at the Tower of Henry VI (1422–61 and 1470–1) in 1471 elicited differing stories even from contemporary chroniclers and soon created much speculation about the involvement of that most infamous figure in the Tower's history, Richard, Duke of

Gloucester, later Richard III (1483–5). Writing a hundred or so years later, the historian Raphael Holinshed concluded that Gloucester '(to the extent that his brother king Edward might reign in more surety) murdered the said king Henry with a dagger', only then to mention as an aside that others claimed that he had died in prison of melancholy.

Perhaps the most bizarre form of execution that took place only a few years later was that of George, Duke of Clarence, for high treason against his brother Edward IV (1461–70 and 1471–83). Official accounts relate that he was privately put to death at the Tower. One contemporary adds that he was drowned on the orders of the Lord High Steward, in a butt of Malmsey wine – his particular favourite. By the time this story had been included in Sir Thomas More's somewhat biased *History of Richard III* the murder was firmly placed at the hands of Richard of Gloucester, once again. Small wonder that over the years such a colourful tale became embellished so that in the more expansive guidebooks of the early Victorian era we find a detailed description of the Bowyer Tower, where suppos-

edly this murder took place, complete with a trap door and secret passage.

By the end of the 16th century some of the earliest first-hand accounts of visitors to the Tower came to be written down. These early tourists did not dwell on the Tower's role as a prison even though its more unfortunate inmates were still visible during the period. The German Paul Hentzner visiting in 1598 noted that the Tower was the place of execution of Anne Boleyn and the imprisonment of the young Princess Elizabeth but did not hear any of the dramatic detail that might be expected so short a time after these infamous events took place. Other contemporary visitors mention being shown the axe in the Lieutenant's lodgings and certain 'dungeons' though they give no detail of what or where these were.

The reader longs for an insider's account by one so observant as Samuel Pepys, who was briefly imprisoned in 1679–80. Sadly his diary does not reach that point and even an encounter in his rooms there over dinner with John Evelyn reveals nothing of his circumstances. For more dramatic versions of these events the people turned to the popular arts.

Archbishop Cranmer taken to the Tower, 1856, by Frederick Goodall. Victorian painters created their own melodramatic versions of scenes from history, rich in closely observed details of costume and setting. Goodall made studies at the Tower where he was put off by the stench of the moat.

*Miniature of Lady
Catherine Grey
by Levina Teerlinc,
c1555–60.*

Catherine Grey
(1540–68)

PRISONER: 1561–3

Lady Catherine Grey was the sister to Lady Jane, and led almost as tragic a short life. Granddaughter to Mary Tudor, younger sister of Henry VIII, she was of royal blood and posed a threat to the insecure accession of Mary I and Elizabeth I.

In 1554, she learnt that her father, sister and brother-in-law had all been executed after the ill-starred attempt to place her elder sister, Jane, on the throne in place of Mary I. Afterward, despite her fears, Catherine enjoyed a brief period of security as Mary I showed a willingness to put the past behind her. In the happiness of her impending marriage to Philip of Spain and in expectation that she would soon produce her own children, Mary forgave the Greys, and Catherine and her younger sister, Mary, were appointed Maids of Honour.

On the succession of Elizabeth I, however, Catherine once again found that her royal blood defined her as a threat to the new queen. Catherine's clandestine marriage to Edward Seymour, Earl of Hertford, in 1560, did not help. The Seymours were well known for their political ambition and together the young couple provided an alternative political faction for any disenfranchised members of the Elizabethan court. Elizabeth learnt of the marriage only when Catherine's pregnancy became too obvious to conceal. Both Catherine and her husband were sent to the Tower in September 1561 and ordered into separate lodgings. Their marriage was then declared illegal. Catherine gave birth to a son, Edward, who was christened in the parlour of Edward Warner, the Lieutenant of the Tower.

The Lieutenant continued to let the young couple meet in secret and in 1562 Catherine became the only Tower state prisoner to conceive during her imprisonment. A second son, Thomas, was born in 1563. The Earl of Hertford was fined £15,000 (later reduced to £3,000) for 'deflowering a virgin of the Royal Blood' and flouting the terms of his imprisonment.

In 1563, plague ravaged London and the most important state prisoners were released from the Tower into house arrest. Catherine and the infant Thomas were sent to her uncle John Grey's home in Essex; Edward and their eldest son to his mother's house at Hanworth. Husband and wife never saw each other again. Catherine died from tuberculosis in 1568, still under house arrest.

Sir Walter Ralegh (1552?–1618)

Sir Walter Ralegh, a favourite of Elizabeth I, was imprisoned in the Tower three times. His first confinement was for five weeks in 1592 for marrying one of Elizabeth's ladies-in-waiting, Elizabeth Throckmorton, without the Queen's permission. His wife was also sent to the Tower but they were kept apart.

On the second occasion, Ralegh was held in the Bloody Tower for 13 years, from 1603 to 1616, on a charge of treason, for allegedly conspiring against James I (1603–25) and trying to place the King's cousin, Lady Arbella Stuart, on the throne. His involvement in this so-called 'Main Plot' was never convincingly proved and he was dramatically reprieved by the King on the day set for his execution.

As a gentleman prisoner, Ralegh's conditions in the Bloody Tower were generally comfortable. He was allowed three servants and, for a time, his wife and son, Walter, were permitted to stay with him. The parish register of the Chapel Royal of St Peter ad Vincula records the birth of a second son, Carew, at the Tower in February 1605. In 1605–6, the interior of the Bloody Tower was partitioned to provide more living space for the family and their servants. Ralegh had an allowance from the Exchequer for basic necessities such as food and clothing. These funds were obtained from the confiscation of his estate and the sale of his possessions. The former Captain of the Guard, Governor of Jersey, and High Sheriff and Lieutenant of Cornwall had

Sir Walter Ralegh, attributed to the monogrammist 'H', 1588.

been stripped of his honours and spent much of his imprisonment worrying about the reduced circumstances of his family.

Ralegh exercised in the garden beside the Bloody Tower and along the wall outside his room. James I's ministers complained about the 'lawless liberty of the Tower' and his privileges were sometimes withdrawn. In spite of his relative comfort, Ralegh's health and morale were often poor and in 1603 he made an unsuccessful attempt at suicide.

Ralegh's travels to Virginia and Guiana during Elizabeth I's reign had left him with an interest in exotic plants from the New World. The Lieutenant of the Tower allowed him to grow several of these in his garden, including tobacco. He was also permitted to experiment with brewing herbal medicines in a converted hen-house close by. Ralegh's 'Balsam of Guiana'

was widely known in London society. He also wrote poetry and studied widely, including chemistry and history. His most substantial work, *The History of the World* was intended for Henry, Prince of Wales, who supported him against his father, James I. However, after the Prince's premature death in 1612, Ralegh only completed the first volume (published in 1614) and the great work remained unfinished at his own execution.

Ralegh was released from the Tower in March 1616 in order to undertake an expedition for James I, to Guiana, in search of gold. The expedition was a disaster and Ralegh was charged with deliberately inciting war between Spain and England. In August 1618 he began his third and final imprisonment in the Tower, this time in the Beauchamp Tower, and was executed on 29 October 1618 in Old Palace Yard, Westminster.

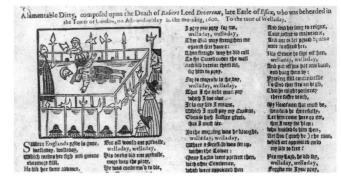

Playwrights, playing cards and painters

Literary authors, as well as historians, have touched on momentous episodes in the Tower's past whilst they were still within living memory. Writing in the early 1500s a young Thomas More – later a victim of Henry VIII (1509–47) at the Tower himself – was determined to establish his own view of events surrounding the death of the 'Princes in the Tower', Edward V and his brother, Richard, Duke of York, when he wrote his *History of Richard III*. This became the principal origin of accounts of Richard's culpability in the princes' murder and was to inspire the most dramatic version of this story found in Shakespeare's play of that name:

[Queen Elizabeth to the Duchess of York]

Stay, yet look back with me unto the Tower.
Pity, you ancient stones, those tender babes
Whom envy hath immur'd within your walls,
Rough cradle for such pretty little ones.
Rude ragged nurse, old sullen playfellow
For tender princes, use my babies well.
So foolish sorrows bid your stones farewell.

[Act IV, scene I]

Shakespeare's plays dealing with British history reinforced the Tudor perspective of the turbulent times after the Wars of the Roses and he created high drama from the real but sometimes clouded events when the Tower served as both prison and scene of regicide. He also evoked the Tower as a setting for equally momentous national events in his *Richard II* and *Henry VI* (Pts 1 & 3). In a cruel twist of fate, More's own life was dramatised in a contemporary play by a group of leading playwrights, including Shakespeare, with the Tower once again providing the setting for an emotional scene of imprisonment and execution. These plays helped to build the popular perception of the Tower as a state prison, at a time when it regularly served that important political purpose.

The Earl of Essex's equally dramatic exit at the Tower following his failed rebellion in 1601 was quickly commemorated in popular ballads of the day and later taken up in an early romance, *A Secret History of the Most Renowned Queen Elizabeth and the Earl of Essex* published in the 17th century. Though not great literature, these publications were widely circulated in print, unlike the plays of Shakespeare in the early 17th century, and helped to promote the common image of the Tower as the setting for bloody events in English history.

More common still were sets of early illustrated playing cards which include some of these events as crude woodcuts. The scenes they depicted were completely imagined, relying on the iconic symbol of the White Tower or popular stories passed on by oral tradition. Though unreliable as any form of visual record, images of this type were significant because they represent how the Tower was viewed by the majority of the populace, many of whom could not read nor had any access to books.

The development of engravings as a cheap and accessible way of commemo-

This woodcut from a cheap ballad sheet is a near-contemporary view of the execution of the Earl of Essex (1601). Although not drawn from life it records details reasonably accurately.

A late 17th-century playing card from a set decorated with scenes of Tower imprisonment and execution, showing Guy Fawkes in his cell. It provides a glimpse of how ordinary people imagined such infamous events.

A contemporary engraving recording crowds gathered for the execution of the Royalist Earl of Strafford, in 1641 by Wenceslaus Hollar. This image is a powerful reminder of the Tower as a place of public spectacle as well as state prison.

rating important events naturally led to a number of execution or imprisonment scenes from the Tower being recorded, or in some cases imagined. These could be reliable and based on a degree of first-hand observation by the artist or they could be reworkings of images already in circulation, published often in illustrated broadsheets, the precursor of the modern newspaper. What is clear from many of these is that in the late 17th and 18th centuries commercial artists rarely had access to draw in the towers and other buildings where prisoners were actually kept.

By the later 18th century such events at the Tower were becoming increasingly exceptional and were treated as spectaculars. Around this time a new kind of image of the Tower arose. This came out of a school of painting that tackled subjects in British history for the first time. The styles of such artists were diverse, some classical and some reflecting the rise of the Romantic movement in the arts. A particularly important new source of subject material was the theatre, where a revival of interest in Shakespeare was taking place. Inspired by celebrity actors like David Garrick, who in 1743 had introduced a greater naturalism into his leading roles, a new genre of painting actors in character evolved. These could be single figures posed in the almost contemporary cos-

tume of the day or whole stage scenes. Such paintings were high art, aimed at the most influential levels of society. However, the theatre itself was booming and was one of the few forms of culture shared by very mixed audiences. Consequently, these new, more naturalistic productions of Shakespeare, in particular, would have been widely appreciated. Over the same period the first illustrated editions of his collected works appeared. Their engravings were highly popular and could prove lucrative, whereas for most painters creating unfamiliar images from Britain's history was not often commercially successful. Their work did find a vociferous audience with critics attending the new exhibition salons of the 1760s.

A typical example of this was the portrait painter James Northcote, who began exploring Shakespeare's subject material in 1785 when he created the scene from *Richard III* of *Edward V and his Brother Murdered*. In his memoirs he reveals a certain anxiety about the success of this picture that he showed in private to the President of the Royal Academy, Sir Joshua Reynolds. The great man appeared to damn the work with faint praise, but Northcote was delighted to find out that after their meeting Reynolds had spoken of nothing else all day. Not unusually for the spirit of the age, the artist had based

Right: *Alderman Boydell opened his private gallery of paintings from Shakespeare in 1789. Such salons allowed artists like Northcote to reach their most influential audiences, including royalty and the aristocracy. Drawing by Francis Wheatley, 1790.*

one of the assassins on a rough-looking beggar he had brought to his studio. With this picture Northcote claimed some credit for the inspiration for the most influential scheme to produce an illustrated Shakespeare volume to the highest standards, produced by Alderman John Boydell in the following year. Although this was eventually a commercial failure, the prints proving too ambitious to bankroll the venture, it did encourage the creation of the largest number of original pictures from Shakespeare by the leading painters of the day. Not only were these all engraved for sale, but Boydell created a picture gallery on Pall Mall where they were readily accessible to the paying public. Over nearly two decades more than 70 works were created including four Tower scenes from *Richard III* and *Henry VI Part I* by Northcote. He also created an equally melodramatic image of Lady Jane Grey in prison. Other artists who tackled these popular Gothick scenes included William Hogarth, William Blake and Henry Fuseli, all of whom imagined Richard III's dream scene, where the King is plagued by the ghosts of his victims.

However, it was not in England that the most memorable Romantic images of the Tower as a prison were created but in France, where an even more fervent interest in Shakespeare took hold in the arts

Above left: William Hogarth created the first painting from Shakespeare in 1745, with this portrait of the actor David Garrick in his highly influential role as Richard III.

Above right: The late 18th-century artist James Northcote was one of the first to create disturbing scenes based on Shakespeare's Richard III. In this painting of 1785 he graphically imagines the murder of the Princes in the Tower.

after years of disinterest. Championed by giants like Hugo and Berlioz it was not long before painters turned to these subjects too. Furthermore, the second French revolution in 1830 made dramatic scenes from England's more distant turbulent past all the more appealing to a nation once again in turmoil. That same year Paul Delaroche created the first of his great scenes from English history, *The Children of Edward IV*.

This young painter was carving a successful career from historical scenes, with a sharp eye for details of costume and scene setting. Though not factually accurate his scenes were far more convincing in their attempt to evoke the past than what had gone before. He also showed a particularly acute sense of drama, creating

a feeling of pathos and suspense that appealed to the audience of the day. In his version of the story of the Princes in the Tower he dispensed with the need for the ghastly murderers' presence, choosing instead to merely suggest their terrible fate by the glow of light from under the door. Delaroche produced several versions of his picture and it was later engraved, gaining a wider audience. He went on to repeat the success a few years later with a subject that was to become a fixation with artists and authors in the 19th century, the imprisonment and death of Lady Jane Grey. Transferring the real execution scene from Tower Green to a gloomy interior where the young Queen stands out, dressed in white, Delaroche created one of the most powerful images of this genre. No matter that he had never seen the Tower for himself for there were by now plenty of accounts published for him and artists like him to draw upon. He soon returned to the Tower for inspiration when he painted the Royalist opponent, Lord Strafford, on his way to his execution as he received a blessing from the arms of Archbishop Laud, whom he depicted stretching through the bars of his own cell. Of course there were no cells with bars to be found at the Tower by this time.

The middle of the 19th century produced a wealth of such images from history including quite a number of famous prisoners of the Tower. Many of these were first exhibited at the Royal Academy's annual exhibition and later engraved. Victorian artists were inspired by the critical success of pioneers like Delaroche or popular historical novelists. Their names include Solomon Hart, (1839, 1860), JR Herbert (1844), John Cross (1850), Frederick Goodall (1856), WJ Grant (1861), William Yeames (1863, 1867) and John Everett Millais (1878), mostly very successful artists capable of satisfying the growing demand for scenes from British history

in a realistic manner, which reflected a society obsessed with material values. Their works were certainly detailed in their observation though rarely authentic in depicting particular historical events. What these artists all intended for their public was to extract the moral significance from the scenes. They were also contributing to Britain's growing sense of nationalism, which was firmly founded on a sense of its own history.

Guards and guides

Who is to prevent some thousands each with a shilling from going there if they please and when there from doing what they please?

[The Duke of Wellington in 1837 as Constable of the Tower.]

It was not until the start of Queen Victoria's (1837–1901) reign that same year that the popular experience of the Tower as a gruesome prison began to reach a much larger audience. By the 18th century there was a well worn system for showing individuals or small groups around the fortress, led by a Yeoman Warder for a gratuity, which was expected at each attraction. At that time the warders were still active prison guards – and no doubt could

furnish vivid descriptions of some of the more notorious events in the Tower's history. Zacharias von Uffenbach, arriving in 1710 reported, 'Anyone who wishes to enter must... report himself to the Yeoman of the Guard on the right and leave his sword with them. Then one of these English "Schweizer" is sent with him as a guide'. He also made note of seeing 'two prisoners of quality' (Jacobite rebels) walking on Tower Green – hardly the evidence of state punishment promised in his German guidebook.

It was the Tower's buildings, Armouries and Jewel House that were the chief attractions for him as for other early visitors, but he expressed disappointment at not seeing 'the chains and fetters which the Spaniards meant to bind the English', referring to the Spanish Armoury. This was a concoction of genuine weapons associated with the Armada and a number of more dubious devices. It is the only feature of the Tower as state prison that is mentioned in the first guidebooks. From the earliest examples of the 1730s, a succession of these publications adds little to the Tower's darker reputation. The one attraction they nearly all erroneously mention is the Tudor axe which was traditionally held to have been used at the execution of Anne Boleyn, instead of a sword that was her special privilege. It was not until the very end of that century that the guides even mention the remains in the Chapel Royal of those who were executed within the Tower's forbidding walls. Instead it was largely left to the visions of growing numbers of authors of fictional romances or artists to stir the public's imagination on these subjects.

What is not recorded – at least until the very end of the 19th century – is how these guardians of the Tower explained the parts of the fortress that were open to visitors. There seems little doubt that, as witnesses over time to actual imprisonment, execution or even torture, they contributed to the oral history that created many of the Tower's myths and misconceptions. This is certainly the impression given in the growing number of guides to London published by the beginning of the 19th century, which often gloss over known fact in preference to repeating more colourful scenes from the past.

Growing public curiosity at the Tower as state prison was at once both checked and given further stimulation when in 1821 the antiquarian John Bayley produced the first scholarly account of the building's history since John Stow's *Survey of London* of 1598. Working in the Tower Record Office, with state papers to hand, he was ideally placed to provide a corrective to this growing romanticised view of the castle. His full description of the various buildings is admirably accurate for its day, with a wealth of architectural detail, and was illustrated with Frederick Nash's ele-

gant views and plans. In dealing with stories of imprisonment he cites the various sources and is careful to correct popular misconceptions. However, when the site of a famous incarceration is touched upon even he cannot resist speculating on the evidence before him: writing of the well-known 'cell' leading off the chapel crypt in the White Tower he claims that 'there can be little doubt that these gloomy apartments were originally designed as prisons' and repeats the apocryphal story of Ralegh writing his *History of the World* in that windowless space.

Bayley's *History* was no mere guide, running into two volumes and produced quite lavishly. In the second part, published four years later, he devotes himself 'to biographical anecdote', dealing entirely with an account of distinguished prisoners. One especially important contribution was a thorough, illustrated gazetteer to all the carved prisoners' inscriptions that had been recently uncovered in the Beauchamp Tower – at that time not accessible to visitors. Though the book was a tremendous advance in scholarship the very wealth of detail on the subject was soon to spark off the greatest wave of creative interest in the less seemly side of the Tower's history. The first response came a few years later in a smaller, rival publication by the distinguished topographical writer John Britton collaborating with the archaeologist and topographer EW Brayley. In their preface they claimed to be meeting a need for a new publication after the arrangement of new displays in the Armouries that had taken

CONCILIVM SEPTEM NOBILIVM ANGLORVMCONIVRANTIVM IN NECEM IACOBI · I ·
MAGNÆ · BRITANNIÆ · REGIS · TOTIVSQ · ANGLICI · CONVOCATI PARLEMENTI ·

Bates

Robert
Winter

Christopher
Wright

Iohn
Wright

Thomas
Percy

Guido
Fawkes

Robert
Catesby

Thomas
Winter

Guy Fawkes (1570–1606)

The Gunpowder Plot Conspirators, 1605, published by Crispijn van de Passe the Elder.

Memorial in the Queen's House on Tower Green, commemorating the discovery of the Gunpowder Plot.

PRISONER: 1605–6

In the early hours of 5 November 1605, Guy Fawkes was found in the cellars beneath the Houses of Parliament with 36 barrels of gunpowder, 'three matches, and all other instruments fit for blowing up the powder, ready upon him'. His intention was to kill James I, his queen and his heir, as well as Parliament.

Fawkes and his co-conspirators – among them Robert Catesby, Thomas Percy, Ambrose Rookewoode and Sir Everard Digby – wanted an end to the persecution of Catholics and planned to start an armed rebellion in the aftermath of the explosion. However, details of the plot leaked out and the King was shown an anonymous letter warning that 'they shall receive a terrible blow this parliament and yet they shall not see who hurts them'.

Fawkes was taken to the Tower. The leading conspirators were soon tracked to Holbeach House in Staffordshire, where some were shot dead attempting to avoid capture. The survivors joined Fawkes in the Tower. Some were held in the Wall Walk towers where their inscriptions can still be seen, carved into the walls. Fawkes was interrogated by the Privy Council, most persistently by William Waad, the Lieutenant of the Tower, who had many years of experience in interrogating Catholics and a reputation as one of the chief persecutors of Catholics in England.

Fawkes stood up to questioning for several days, revealing nothing. It was then that torture was considered. According to one account, the rack was 'only offered and showed to him', but some people believe otherwise. The difference between his signatures that appeared on his confessions before and after interrogation has led some to conclude that his writing hand had been badly damaged by being stretched on the rack.

Fawkes was accused of conspiring to murder the King and his family, to stir rebellion in the kingdom, to subvert religion and to bring in strangers to invade the commonwealth. He eventually confessed to all charges and received the sentence of death. On 30 and 31 January 1606, Fawkes and his fellow conspirators were trussed up. One by one, they were strapped on to hurdles and dragged through the streets to their execution. Their bodies were hung, drawn and quartered, and parts were displayed in various locations around London as a warning to others.

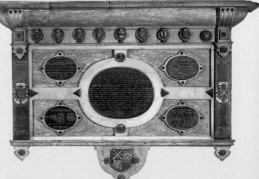

A caricature of the popular Victorian novelist William Harrison Ainsworth, by Edward Linley Sambourne, published in the journal Punch *in 1881 as* The Greatest axe-and-neck-romancer of his time.

place in the 1820s. These had been partly in response to increasing expectations from visitors and partly to antiquarians' increased role in running the Tower. Their book largely turned to Bayley for authority. However, they did add to its scholarship. When dealing with historical accounts of such controversial subjects such as the death of the Princes in the Tower they are scrupulous in comparing, for instance, Thomas More's version with earlier sources as well as introducing more recent discussion by Horace Walpole on the subject in his *Historic Doubts* on More's biography. Walpole was one of the first historians to question seriously the Richard III story.

A historical romance

This move towards greater historical accuracy in print, instead of dwelling on more prurient aspects of the Tower's history suddenly swung in the opposite direction with the appearance of a romance or historical novel, *The Tower of*

London by William Harrison Ainsworth, which appeared in 1840. His book can be seen as perhaps the pivotal point in the making of the image of the Tower as a prison, when creative imagination began not only to shape how people looked at the Tower but even how it was presented to growing numbers of visitors.

Ainsworth was a contemporary and acquaintance of Dickens, though he represents what has become known as the 'Newgate School' of novelists, who had a reputation for prolific, if not very moralistic tales from history that were liberally littered with villainous characters based on popular accounts from the notorious county gaol at Newgate. *The Tower of London* managed to combine the background detail of Bayley's worthy study of the Tower with Ainsworth's own love of historical romance. The book was long on imaginative scene setting and short on historical accuracy. His most ingenious device was to cloak the gripping tale of Lady Jane Grey and Queen Mary I in all the detail of the Tower, adding a generous number of invented subplots. The novel was illustrated with over 40 engravings by the leading cartoonist and illustrator, George Cruickshank, which undoubtedly led to its popularity as it came out in cheap instalments in a magazine.

Ainsworth declared that he wished to show the Tower 'in its triple light of a Palace, a Prison and a Fortress' though it was as a prison that it excited him most. He was open about how his story was contrived to 'introduce every relic of the old pile... so that no part should remain

The Duke of Monmouth (1649–85)

PRISONER: 1685

James Scott, Duke of Monmouth was the illegitimate son of Charles II and his mistress, Lucy Walters. He was executed on Tower Hill on 15 July 1685 for rebelling against his uncle, the new king, James II.

James, Duke of York, Charles II's brother, had converted to Catholicism in 1672, which led to an attempt by Parliament to exclude him from the succession. Many felt that Charles should legitimise his beloved bastard son so that the crown would pass to a Protestant but the King would not comply and Charles was succeeded by his brother. Four months after James became king, he faced a rebellion by the Duke of Monmouth.

JAMES D. OF MONMOUTH.

Monmouth landed in south-west England in July 1685 from the Netherlands. Using the advantage of surprise, he attacked James II's army at Sedgemoor on 5 July. But the King's superior troops massacred Monmouth's ill-trained rabble 'until the soldiers were weary of killing'. Monmouth himself was captured, disguised as a shepherd.

While Monmouth was taken to London, savage reprisals were carried out against his followers in a series of trials known as the 'Bloody Assizes', which were overseen by the exceptionally severe Judge Jeffreys. Jeffreys declared that anyone who had recognised Monmouth as king could be hanged without trial and without mercy. Some 300 men were executed and many more were sold into slavery. Monmouth himself was taken to the Tower, where he was made to sign a paper expressing his sorrow for what he had done, and was beheaded soon after. It took 'five Chopps' of the axe to sever his head from his body.

James Scott, Duke of Monmouth and Buccleuch, possibly after William Wissing, c1683.

A 17th-century German engraving depicting the execution of the Duke of Monmouth in 1685.

unillustrated'. What he certainly did achieve was to draw attention to the fact that some of the most significant sites of the Tower associated with imprisonment, namely the Beauchamp Tower and parts of the White Tower, had long been inaccessible to the public. He also decried the sorry state of the medieval parts of the Tower that he saw as ruined by the later additions of the armouries, storehouses and manufactories.

Much of Ainsworth's book is pure fiction and the source of several Tower myths that have been repeated endlessly. For instance he describes the arrival of Princess Elizabeth in captivity as set in a torture chamber, 'which was lighted by a dull lamp from the roof, and furnished as before with numberless hideous implements – each seemingly to have been recently employed' wherein she finds the tortured conspirator Sir Thomas Wyatt stripped half-naked.

Cruickshank's illustrations, whilst undoubtedly based on visits to sketch at the Tower, are full of exaggeration and Victorian melodrama and are not particularly impressive works of art. In this they are not helped by the cartoon-like quality of his figures. What cannot be denied though is their influence on other artists and writers when viewed alongside

Ainsworth's often purple prose. Their work went on to reach an even wider popular audience through cheap penny plays that openly plagiarised the book. Under titles such as *The Tower of London or The Death, Omen and Fate of Lady Jane Grey* (Thomas Higgins and Thomas Lacy; produced at the City of London Theatre in December 1840) they romped through the raciest parts of Ainsworth's book borrowing his and Cruickshank's scenery, such as 'Gothic Apartment[s]' where clinking chains and bolts being shot accompanied the actors' words. A second play managed to combine *The Tower of London* with Dumas's *Marie Tudor* and included a comic scene of Ainsworth's where three giant warders, called Og, Gog and Magog are engaged in a bawdy romp with a lady of the Tower. A much later and higher quality, but no less inventive, recycling of Ainsworth's romance came in 1888 with Gilbert and Sullivan's operetta *The Yeoman of the Guard*. Originally to be called *The Tower of London*, its librettist WS Gilbert was initially inspired by an advertisement at a train station, which featured a picture of the Tower. For this unhistorical entertainment he bothered to visit the Tower to sketch notes on the guards there.

Ainsworth's original book was an enormous success and publishers offered to

Princess Elizabeth confronting Thomas Wyatt in the torture chamber. Illustration by George Cruickshank from Ainsworth's The Tower of London, *1840. Cruickshank visited the Tower on several occasions to find his settings for the novelist's largely imaginary scenes.*

produce a monthly sequel in editions of upwards of 20,000 copies. Later in life Ainsworth did produce two more books on similar themes but by that time public interest had begun to wane, perhaps in part due to a fall in the popularity of the Tower as a growing tourist attraction after the boom in the 1840s and 1850s. By this time the mythology of the Tower as prison was irresolutely established as a part of the national monument

Building on the myth

During the 19th century the Tower authorities gradually responded to increased public interest, as well as pressure from reformers. From the late 1830s they began to improve both access to the Tower's more famous sights and also what was offered to visitors once inside. This all happened under the disparaging eye of the Constable, the Duke of Wellington, who was most reluctant to see the Tower change from an active military garrison to a public spectacle. These changes can be followed through later Tower guidebooks and the increasing number of cheap guides for tourists.

At the time that the price of entrance was dropped two-thirds to one shilling (still a substantial amount), the old Spanish

Yeoman Warders were in the habit of demonstrating torture and execution instruments to visitors, as this view of 1871 shows. This satirical scene includes the former Prime Minister, Benjamin Disraeli before the axe, watched by John Bull.

Armoury of 1688, with its instruments of torture, had moved to the crypt of the Chapel of St John in the White Tower, where it became known as Queen Elizabeth's Armoury. Here the axe was displayed again, though in the first official history of the Tower its doubtful connection with Anne Boleyn was at least admitted. This change also gave the public access to parts of the White Tower for the first time and with it the cramped room that became known as Sir Walter Ralegh's cell. An initial quadrupling of visitors from around 10,000 to over 40,000 in just two years from 1837 encouraged authors to publish more information about the Tower's history. Several of these gradually added to the stock of prisoner locations to be seen, repeating tales that had been corrected by Bayley and other antiquarians years before, such as the imprisonment of Princess Elizabeth in the Bell Tower. Subterranean passages, as featured in Ainsworth, were alluded to without anything 'new' to show to visitors. In the second half of the century a number of additional spurious torture implements had been entered into Queen Elizabeth's Armoury, including a model rack and the so-called headsman's mask. A later curator even suggested that the notorious Scavenger's Daughter had been bought for

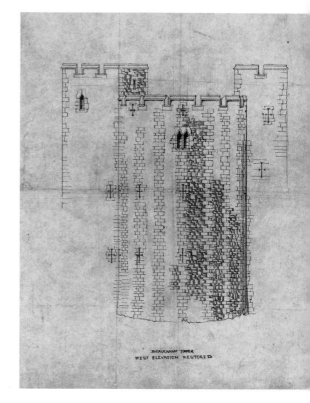

the Tower in the 1820s. Visitors were not disappointed by such revelations, as the warders continued to provide a tour of these items that was very engaging. For years they were able to handle these dubious instruments and were sometimes encouraged to try them out – up to a point.

As Ainsworth had rightly pointed out, the most important evidence of the Tower as a prison – the Beauchamp Tower with its prisoners' inscriptions – remained closed until the Office of Works (as it became) in charge of repairs to the Tower commissioned the gothic-revival architect Anthony Salvin to clear houses around the tower and restore its castellated appearance. Salvin was the ideal choice because of his experience working on several castles previously and his prodigious talent for designing in convincing historic styles. The Beauchamp Tower opened in 1854, where a special souvenir guide could be purchased from a Yeoman Warder. The following year the Board of Ordnance merged with the War Office, as the supply

problems in the Crimean War were dealt with. This gradually led to the release of more areas of the Tower as workshops and stores moved elsewhere. Similarly, another institution that had occupied large areas of the Tower, the Record Office, soon moved away to larger premises. Over the next 20 years or so Salvin continued to clear away more recent buildings from the medieval fabric, often in quite a ruthless manner that was later derided. Former prisoner locations, the Salt, St Thomas's, Wakefield, Martin, Bloody and Cradle towers were all also restored by him in this manner. Work was continued in other areas after him by a lesser architect, John Taylor.

The important result of this programme of largely public works was to reinvent the Tower as a medieval castle, which would at long last match up to the vision that had been created by historians, writers and artists. No matter that much of it was inauthentic or that the lost cells long talked about turned out either not to exist or when uncovered during

Above left: *View of the Beauchamp Tower from Tower Hill before restoration, by Charles Tomkins, 1798.*

Above right: *The Beauchamp Tower's restoration as completed by Anthony Salvin in 1854, the first of his projects to return the Tower of London to its medieval appearance. For the first time the public were able to view the many inscriptions carved by prisoners in this tower.*

clearances were found to have much less sinister explanations.

One irony of the way in which the Tower was 'medievalised', with crenellations restored, arrow loops repaired and doorways returned to their gothic forms, was that it looked more like a castle-prison than ever, when its use a prison was practically over. At the same time as Salvin's work was undertaken at the Tower, a number of architects were designing new, more humane, prisons along the lines of reform suggested by John Howard in the later 18th century (see page 10). Several of these even took the form of a mock-fortress for their entrances, such as

In 1877 the Chapel Royal of St Peter ad Vincula was finally cleared of its Georgian paraphernalia and at Queen Victoria's insistence the first memorial to the victims of execution within the Tower was installed in the Sanctuary pavement.

The scaffold site was first marked out for visitors in 1866, though the actual execution site probably varied on each occasion.

Holloway and Wandsworth prisons in London.

Two more important changes to the castle were wrought in the latter part of the 19th century which further added to the presentation of the Tower as a state prison, as much as a fortress. The traditional site of the scaffold on Tower Green was marked in paving and railed off in 1866, on a site remarkably close to that suggested by the illustrations in Ainsworth's book. (In reality there had been no permanent scaffold site within the Tower during the 16th century when most of the executions there took place.) Attention then turned to the Chapel Royal of St Peter ad Vincula, which had disappointed writers, and presumably visitors too, for many years because there was little to show for the tombs of the executed queens and nobility of England buried there. Salvin prepared a plan to clear out all the paraphernalia of 18th-century ministry that was eventually carried out by 1877. Queen Victoria herself demanded the careful reburial of her royal ancestors' and others' remains and a small memorial to them.

There was no written master plan for these works, but rather the coming together of general expectations of what the Tower should look like and practical expediency over the years. This followed the development of the Tower from a largely industrial and military building into a national tourist attraction. A combination of enlightened officers in charge at various times and external political pressure gradually brought about

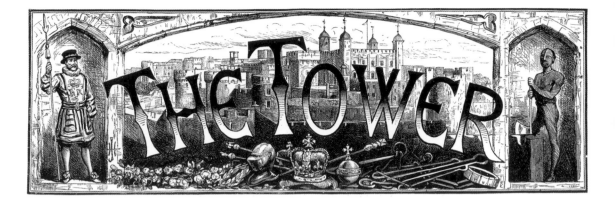

these changes in this way. An interesting parallel existed at Hampton Court Palace, that other great setting for Tudor intrigues. Like the Tower, it was greatly opened up to visitors at the beginning of Queen Victoria's reign in 1837–8, with direct encouragement from the new queen. As at the Tower, the researches of another antiquarian writer, Edward Jesse, provided the direction for public works architects who returned parts of the palace to his personal vision of the past.

The popular image of the Tower as a state prison and place of execution was built up in this way over the centuries, an amalgam of historical record, oral tradition and more modern myth-making. Towards the end of the 19th century this image was very much established and indeed played upon in promoting the Tower, whether for the causes of tourism, education or to raise its profile to secure funds for improvements. Even when it returned briefly to its function as a prison during the First World War, it remained open to visitors.

This image lived on into the 20th century, now in the form of popular fiction and history books, such as Lytton Strachey's *Elizabeth and Essex* in the 1920s and Josephine Tey's historical whodunit, *The Daughter of Time*, about the Princes in the Tower, in the 1960s. It was also exploited in the new media of film in the 1930s (*Elizabeth and Essex* and *The Tower of London*, both released in 1939) and inevitably later taken up by television, most notably in the BBC's 'The Six Wives of Henry the Eighth'.

These myths and stories are still enjoyed by the millions of people who visit the Tower each year. The main difference between them and their predecessors in earlier centuries is that today visitors are able to place this image alongside an unparalleled wealth of published and broadcast historical information and analysis.

Illustrated magazines and guidebooks of the Victorian era promulgated the idea of the Tower as first-and-foremost a state prison, though it had long since relinquished that role. The Graphic, *1885.*

Advertisement for the 1939 horror movie, The Tower of London, *starring Basil Rathbone and Boris Karloff. The Tower as a prison has featured in the sets of numerous historic dramas and films, usually conjured up by the imagination of art directors.*

Lord Mayor Brass Crosby, engraving by W Dickinson after a lost painting by Robert Edge Pine, 1771. The White Tower can be seen in the background of this portrait and its companion.

Alderman Richard Oliver, by Robert Edge Pine, painted whilst at the Tower in 1771. Pine himself supported their radical cause and eventually left Britain for America

Brass Crosby (1725–93) and Richard Oliver (1734?–84)

PRISONERS: 1771

Lord Mayor Brass Crosby and Richard Oliver, a prominent Alderman of the City of London were imprisoned for several weeks at the Tower in a struggle for power between Parliament and the City of London.

Brass Crosby was a prominent lawyer from the north west of England, who established his political position both as a Member of Parliament and in the City, where he became Prime Warden of the Worshipful Company of Goldsmiths, before being elected Lord Mayor in 1770. His fellow Alderman, Richard Oliver, became MP for the City. Both men were supporters of new social causes as well as moves towards greater civil liberties.

At the time the English press was regularly forbidden from reporting debates in the House of Commons, as this breached parliamentary privilege. In March 1771 several newspaper print-ers reported these debates openly for the first time and were arrested. However, Crosby, Oliver and the Chief City Magistrate, John Wilkes (who had himself been imprisoned in the Tower in the 1760s for criticising what he saw as an autocratic government) released two of the printers involved and arrest-ed the parliamentary messenger instead, for violating the printers' rights. As MPs, Crosby and Oliver were then summoned to the Commons to account for their actions. (Wilkes was by this time banished from Parliament after his previous dispute with the Government.) The House duly voted against them and they were sent to the Tower for challenging parliamen-tary authority.

Inside the Tower, Crosby was lodged on the parade ground (now Tower Green) and both men were freely visit-ed by Wilkes and other opposition sup-porters. The Council of the City even offered to provide their food whilst they were imprisoned. Outside, popular sup-port was voiced in doggerel verses pub-lished in dedication to the Lord Mayor:

> Nor thou refuse at freedom's call
> Your dungeon's gloomy path to
> tread,
> Beneath whose blood besprinkled
> wall
> Her champion oft with joy have bled.

It soon became clear that Parliament had no appetite for prosecuting the pair and after several weeks Crosby and Oliver were released without charge. They returned to the Mansion House (the Lord Mayor's official residence) amid a great procession of supporters who pulled along Crosby's carriage, accompanied by gun salutes. It was a victory for Wilkes, the City and the com-mon people.

TORTURE IN THE TOWER

We authorise you to proceed to the further examination of Barker and Bannister, the Duke of Norfolk's servants, upon all points... And if they shall not seem to you to confess plainly their knowledge, then we warrant you to cause them both or either of them to be brought to the rack; and first to move them with fear thereof to deal plainly in their answers, and if that shall not move them, then you shall cause them to be put to the rack, and to find the taste thereof until they shall deal more plainly, or until you shall think meet. And so we remit the whole proceeding to your further discretion, requiring you to use speed herein and to require the assistance of our Lieutenant of the Tower.

[Queen Elizabeth I to her Privy Councillors, 15 September 1571.]

The sinister legend of the Tower

Of all the many uses to which the Tower of London has been put, torture has attracted the largest body of myth and legend, and it has come to dominate the image of the Tower in the popular imagination. Nevertheless, behind the legend is a true story and many of the details of torture in the Tower are well documented by reliable sources.

The story of torture in the Tower of London only occupied a relatively short period of the castle's history, from the 16th to the 17th century, and of the prisoners who were held at the Tower, only a tiny fraction were ever tortured. Torture was essentially a matter of gathering information to be used in law, not a matter of punishing prisoners for bad behaviour. Although prisoners in the Tower could be kept in solitary confinement and deprived of food as part of the routine of their imprisonment, actual *physical* torture was used as part of a deliberate programme of interrogation.

Torture has never been officially recognised in English Law as a means of gaining information. The officers who tortured prisoners in the Tower were acting with the knowledge and authority of the highest levels of government – the Privy Council and the monarch – and they were able to do so because royal servants enjoyed immunity from prosecution. However, in public opinion, torture was never accepted as a fact of life. Protestants and Catholics both complained bitterly about the use of torture by regimes of the other party, praising victims as 'martyrs' and labelling the authorities as 'tyrants' or 'persecutors'. Critics claimed that it was ineffective as well as cruel, and that a man on the rack would say anything to be released. From the mid-17th century onwards, torture was effectively abandoned.

The idea of torture in the Tower became a matter of myth and legend long after the instruments of torture had gone. Torture, if it was mentioned at all, was portrayed as a savage foreign invention, and a few surviving instruments were displayed to visitors as 'Spanish'. Myth-making reached its peak in the 19th century, spurred on by novelists of historical

A 17th-century engraving showing the Jesuit priest, Alexander Briant (1553–81) who was committed to the Tower and racked in 1581. The method of torture illustrated is fictitious.

romance. For them, such a fortress must have contained a maze of underground passages and secret cells, culminating in the torture chamber itself:

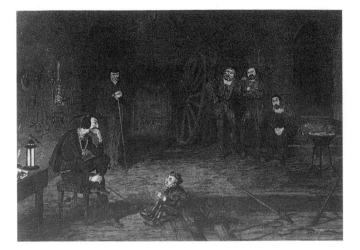

> At the extremity of the passage he found an open door, leading to a small circular chamber, in the centre of which stood a heavy stone pillar. From this pillar projected a long iron bar, sustaining a coil of rope, terminated by a hook. On the ground lay an immense pair of pincers, a curiously-shaped saw and a brasier. In one corner stood a large oaken frame, about three feet high, moved by rollers. At the other was a ponderous wooden machine like a pair of stocks.

> Against the wall stood a broad hoop of iron, opening in the middle with a hinge – a horrible instrument of torture named 'The Scavenger's Daughter'...

This description, in Harrison Ainsworth's *The Tower of London*, gives a very good idea of the 'torture chamber' as countless visitors have imagined it. Books and historical films have spread the image far and wide. The reality was different. The historical record does tell us who were the victims and the torturers, what methods were used and how well they worked, where exactly the prisoners were tortured, and what evidence for this story can still be seen in the Tower of London today.

Imprisonment in the Tower

In the 16th and 17th century, the Tower of London was the home of many different organisations of state, including the Ordnance and the Armoury (responsible for storing and supplying armaments), the Royal Mint, the Record Office and even the Royal Menagerie. It was also technically still a royal palace, though its buildings were falling into disrepair. Imprisonment was only one of many functions of the Tower, and prisoners were kept wherever room could be found for them.

Depiction of the torture chamber by George Cruickshank from Ainsworth's The Tower of London, *1840.*

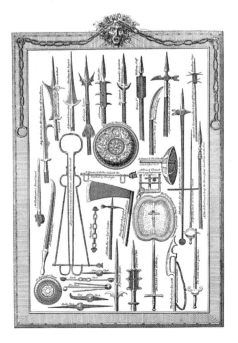

The Spanish Armoury, 1795. This was a notorious display of weapons and torture implements, supposedly intended for English victims of the failed Spanish Armada.

Henry Laurens
(1724–92)

PRISONER: 1780–1

Henry Laurens was the first and last United States citizen to be imprisoned at the Tower. He was held on suspicion of high treason for his part in the American struggle for independence from Great Britain and became a prisoner of state for more than a year.

Laurens's background was anything but revolutionary. A powerful merchant from Charleston in South Carolina, he had made himself wealthy through his trade with native American Indians and also, to his later regret, through the slave trade. As he rose to prominence he was drawn into state politics and became a high-ranking officer in the local militia. At first he was a loyal British colonist but he gradually sided with the Republicans in support of American trade.

When fighting finally broke out in 1775 Laurens found himself at the centre of government in South Carolina and was eventually elected as President of the American Congress. In 1780 Laurens undertook a mission to Holland to seek funds for the American side. However, his merchant vessel was captured by the British and Laurens was taken into custody when incriminating papers he had thrown overboard failed to sink. At first he was treated most cordially but back in London it was immediately evident that he should be treated as a political prisoner. At the time, Parliament feared revolution more than anything else and knew that Laurens's presence in London could prove incendiary. Because Britain did not recognise the United States, Laurens was not grant-

Henry Laurens, painted by Lemuel Frances Abbott, whilst imprisoned at the Tower, 1781 or 1784.

ed diplomatic immunity nor even given the status of a prisoner of war. On 6 October 1780 he was taken to the Tower where he was kept a close prisoner.

Laurens kept an unusually detailed diary of his time at the Tower, which records his view of what was at times rather harsh treatment for the period, when the Tower's role as a prison was diminishing. He was kept indoors in a house on Tower Green belonging to his warder, James Futerell, whom he befriended. The Governor was anxious not to afford Laurens any privileges or allow his presence to excite visitors at the Tower. His rooms were specially barred and he was appalled at being expected to pay not only for his keep, but on one dubious occasion for his own guard as well. Laurens complained: 'Whenever I caught a bird in America, I found a cage and victuals for it.'

Writing secretly in pencil he man-

aged to communicate with his supporters, including the 'rebel' press. Warder Futerell may well have helped him send messages. Although his conditions were later improved he refused to soften to offers of freedom – or even escape – in return for betraying his countrymen.

It was not too long before maintaining this influential but evidently unwell revolutionary at the Tower became an embarrassment for the Government and eventually he was released. His own freedom was bought in return for that of the captured British general Lord Cornwallis, who was none other than Constable of the Tower. Laurens then travelled to be part of negotiations towards the Treaty of Versailles, which ended the War of Independence. He finally returned home in 1784, this time an undisputed American citizen.

Sir Roger Casement (1864–1916)

PRISONER: 1916

As the unsuccessful Easter Rising by Irish Nationalists was taking place in the streets of Dublin in 1916, one of the least likely of the rebel leaders was being sent into custody in the Tower of London. Sir Roger Casement had been a public hero for his stand against slavery and corruption in the rubber plantation economies of the Belgian Congo and Peru. His investigations, his personal bravery and his distinguished British diplomatic career had earned him a knighthood. Yet, Irish-born and a romantic, he harboured strong Irish nationalist views despite his Protestant upbringing. On retiring from the consular service in 1913, he joined the Irish Volunteers and saw the First World War as an ideal opportunity to promote the cause of Ireland.

In Berlin, he courted the German leadership, and in prisoner-of-war camps he tried to persuade Irishmen to desert the British and return with him to fight for an independent Ireland. Few prisoners followed him, but he was given a cache of arms by the Germans. Casement was arrested when landing on the coast of County Kerry on Good Friday, 21 April 1916, intending to support the Easter Rising that came two days later.

Roger Casement was held in the Tower until the preliminary magistrates' enquiry was completed. He was held in the western Casemates, close to the Byward Tower, and was under constant watch as it was feared he would commit suicide.

A campaign in support of Casement was swiftly halted by the British government leaking to opinion-formers and certain members of the press his private diaries, detailing his promiscuous homosexuality. Casement was hanged as a traitor at Pentonville Prison, London, on 3 August 1916. Supporters alleged for decades that the diaries were forgeries, intended to damn him. Forensic investigation has now determined that the diaries are genuine; Casement in the meantime has become an unlikely gay martyr as well as Irish martyr.

Sir Roger Casement photographed by Keogh Brothers Ltd, c1914.

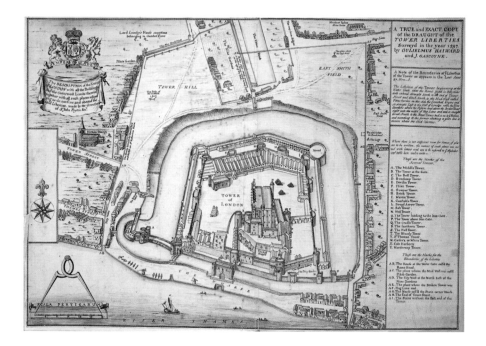

Plan of the Tower in 1597, after Haiward and Gascoyne, showing the numerous towers and workshops within its walls. Many of these buildings were occasionally pressed into use for imprisonment.

Aside from episodes of torture, the routine of imprisonment was certainly lonely and uncomfortable, often anxious and sometimes boring. Numerous prisoners of the 16th and 17th centuries carved graffiti on the walls of rooms and passages, notably in the Beauchamp Tower, the Salt Tower and the Martin Tower. Many of these bear uplifting religious mottos, others merely describe the routine of confinement ('Close prisoner here 8 months, 32 weeks, 224 days, 5376 hours'), while the most part simply give names and dates. Such prisoners clearly had time, the use of their hands and tools of some kind: some of the carvings are so elaborate that the warders must have connived at their creation.

It is clear that most of the prisons in London were not used for torture or interrogation; for that purpose, prisoners were transferred to the Tower, the 'name whereof is terrible abroad', as a Jesuit priest described it. Several government documents mention a particular place within the Tower at which torture was carried out, described as 'the place where the rack remaineth', 'the place of torture' and so on; prisoners were to be brought there from their cells or from interrogation in the Council Chamber. The description left by the Jesuit priest John Gerard tallies with the basement rooms in the White Tower, which then had wooden ceilings supported on wooden posts, and it is almost certain that it was here that torture was carried out:

> We went to the torture room in a kind of solemn procession, the attendants walking ahead with lighted candles. The chamber was underground and dark, particularly near the entrance. It was a vast place and every device and instrument of human torture was there. They pointed out some of them to me and said that I would try them all... Then they took me to a big upright pillar, one of the wooden posts which held the roof of this huge underground chamber.

Also notorious was a cell named 'Little Ease', a space so cramped that the inmate could neither lie down nor stand straight. Cases from the 1550s, 1580s and 1590s show uncooperative prisoners being 'put to the torment' in Little Ease, or being kept there 'two or three days' and then examined further. There has been much speculation about the location of Little

Ease, though the truth may never be known for certain. In 1604, Little Ease was found to be in a very bad condition; it may not have been used again.

The rack and its reconstruction

The principal instrument of torture in the Tower of London was the rack. This device, a bed on which victims were laid and then pulled by ropes from hands and feet, probably had an ancient origin but, at the Tower of London, it was sometimes claimed as the invention of one of the two 15th-century Constables of the Tower to be titled Duke of Exeter, and in the 16th century it was nicknamed 'The Duke of Exeter's Daughter'. Other sources call it 'the brake'.

Not surprisingly, in the 16th and 17th centuries writers speculated about what it might look like, though very few witnesses had actually seen it. The basic principle was well known: the victim's hands and feet were tied to rollers, which were pulled in opposite directions, causing the body to be stretched to the point of pain. The classic image is the engraving from John Foxe's *Acts and Monuments*, published in 1563, showing Cuthbert Simpson being tortured during the reign of Mary I, with torturers standing at the head and foot of the rack, pulling on levers to produce tension.

It is most likely that the Tower rack was a more ingenious piece of engineering. In 1799 the Shakespeare scholar, Isaac Reed, published a description of the remains of a torture device he had located in the stores of the Tower:

It consists of a strong iron frame about 6 feet long, with 3 rollers of wood within it. The middle one of these, which has iron teeth at each end, is governed by 2 stops of iron, and was, probably, that part of the machine which suspended the powers of the rest, when the unhappy sufferer was sufficiently strained by the cords etc to begin confession...

By that time, the rack had been unused for more than a century and several parts had either rotted away or been removed, such as the ropes which fastened the prisoner to the rollers and tied one roller to another, the lever or levers, and the bed on which the victim was stretched out over the rollers. However, by fitting a lever to the central roller and tying the end rollers to it, it has been possible to reconstruct a machine that could be operated by one person. By using the metal teeth, the victim could be held stretched, while

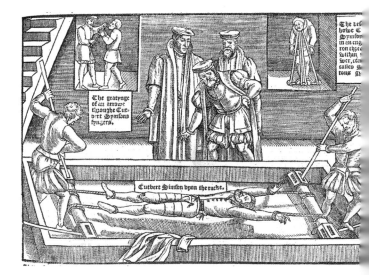

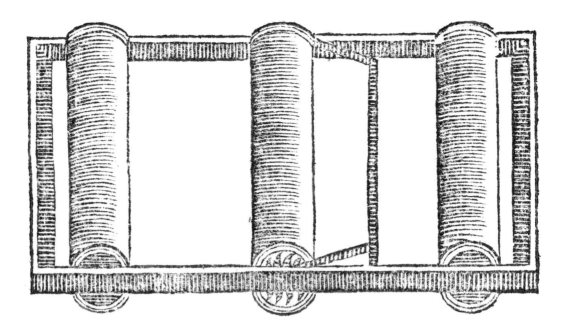

A later 18th-century scholar recovered the remains of the Tower's rack, long since abandoned. It was a surprisingly sophisticated machine considering its crude purpose. Published by Isaac Reed, 1799.

the torturer was ordered from the room. This was an effective way of interrogating a prisoner over matters of state secrecy.

The rack and its victims

Most of the surviving torture warrants which prescribe a particular method specify the rack, running from the case of Thomas Thwaytes in the reign of Henry VIII (1509–47) to that of several anonymous prisoners in 1673, when the 'wrack' was ordered to be prepared (although it may not have been used). It seems clear that the Privy Council saw it as the most effective method. It was standard procedure to show the prisoner the rack first and then to repeat the questions; only if the prisoner remained obstinate should the rack actually be used. With its levers, ropes and rollers, the rack looks more like an instrument of torture than the other devices used in England and it seems likely that several prisoners surrendered before the instrument was used. For example, the Jesuit priest John Hart admitted in December 1581 that while he had 'been at the rack', he had 'endured nothing thereon'.

For those who were tortured on the rack, certain tricks for avoiding suffering were known and passed on between prisoners. In 1556, William Rossey reported how another prisoner, William Staunton, had 'schooled me for the pains of the rack, first to cry a little, then a little more, then to say "In the honour of God be good to me and I will say to you what you will have me say". Then to use yourself in the most dolorous wise that you can'. It was also well known to the authorities that the effect of the rack was increased at a second or third session. Thus in November 1583, Francis Throckmorton, who had refused on the rack to give details of an alleged conspiracy against Elizabeth I (1558–1603) was racked again. The Queen's Secretary wrote 'notwithstanding that great show that he hath made of a Romanist resolution, I suppose that grief of the last torture will suffice without any extremity of racking to make him more conformable than he hath hitherto showed himself'. Throckmorton now answered the questions and was later executed.

One of the most horrific cases of the use of the rack is that of Anne Askew in 1546. Arrested for her outspoken religious views on the Catholic Mass (which she never denied), and after being examined on several occasions before the Council,

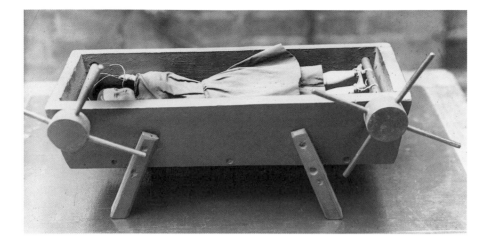

she was brought from Newgate prison to the Tower to be interrogated. When she refused to name others who shared her religious views,

> Then they did put me on the rack because I confessed no ladies or gentlewomen to be of my opinion, and thereon they kept me a long time. And because I lay still and did not cry, my Lord Chancellor and Master Rich took pains to rack me with their own hands till I was nigh dead... Then the Lieutenant caused me to be loosed from the rack: incontinently I swooned, and then they recovered me again...

As the reign of Elizabeth I progressed, the ruthless use of the rack, particularly on Jesuit priests such as Edmund Campion and Alexander Briant, provided ammunition for overseas critics of the English regime. This may partly explain why in the 1590s more writs were issued specifying the use of the manacles.

The Scavenger's Daughter

At the Tower, another type of torture was carried out on the opposite principle to the rack. Whereas the former stretched the body, this caused pain and injury by holding the prisoner in a compressed and contorted position. It was known either after its reputed inventor as Skeffington's Irons or, more imaginatively, as the Scavenger's Daughter.

Unlike the other historic instruments of torture, there is a very strong likelihood that the Scavenger's Daughter has survived in the collection of the Royal Armouries. Since at least the 18th century, an object has been shown as part of the so-called 'Spanish Armoury', a set of devices said to have been taken from the Armada. The object on display, a pair of rods with loops to hold the neck, hands and feet, corresponds closely to a picture in Foxe's *Acts and Monuments* showing the sufferings of Cuthbert Simpson in the Tower in 1557, specifically 'how Cuthbert Simson stood in an engine of iron 3 hours within the Tower, commonly called Scevingtons gyves'.

However, there also exist descriptions and illustrations of another device working by the same principle, but designed differently: as John Hart described it in the 1580s, 'it consists of an iron circle, which compresses the victim's hands, feet and head into a ball'. Something similar was engraved by Richard Verstegan, a critic of Protestant barbarities, in a pamphlet of 1587, and this formed the basis for the most detailed description, published almost a century later in a history of Jesuit saints and martyrs:

Anne Askew (1521–46) was the only woman reputedly tortured at the Tower during the 16th century. This Victorian model of her torture was introduced into the Armouries' displays three centuries later.

The Scavenger's Daughter. Also known as Skeffington's Irons, this type of torture was particularly harmful and only used rarely.

Inscription by Thomas Miagh in the Beauchamp Tower, recording his interrogation and torture in 1581. He was later released.

The body is folded over three ways, with the shins up against the thighs and the thighs against the stomach. The body is locked in two iron bows, whose ends the torturer forces together into a circle, almost crushing the victim's body with a hellish compression. This is a bestial torture, in every way worse than the rack: every part of the body is gripped by savage pain. In some victims, it causes the blood to seep from their fingertips and toes, while for others the rib-cage bursts, and blood flows in a rush from the nostrils and mouth.

The Scavenger's Daughter is rarely mentioned in the documents and the device itself was probably not much used. In December 1580 it was used on two Catholic priests, Luke Kirby and Thomas Cottam, causing Cottam to bleed through the nose; according to an anonymous Catholic writer, after an hour they could endure no more. John Hart's diary states that it was used in September 1582 on John Jetter and in February 1584 on Thomas Nutter. But the best-documented instance is that of the Irishman, Thomas Miagh, charged with being in contact with rebels in Ireland, who was tortured in 1581 first in the Scavenger's Daughter, then on the rack. It may be in connection with the Scavenger's Daughter that Miagh carved on the wall of the Beauchamp Tower, 'By torture straynge my truth was tried, yet of my libertie denied. 1581. Thomas Miagh'.

Detail from a late 16th-century pamphlet showing the Scavenger's Daughter. Victims reportedly could only endure an hour of this torture device.

The manacles

Then they took me to a big upright pillar, one of the wooden posts which held the roof of this huge underground chamber. Driven in to the top of it were iron staples for supporting heavy weights. Then they put my wrists into iron gauntlets and ordered me to climb two or three wicker steps. My arms were then lifted up and an iron bar was passed through the rings of one gauntlet, then through the staple and rings of the second gauntlet. This done, they fastened the bar with a pin to prevent it slipping and then, removing the wicker steps, they left me hanging by my hands and arms fastened above my head.

This describes the third type of torture to be used at the Tower – the manacles. A prisoner held in this way for a long period of time experienced extreme pain and might have difficulty using his hands for a time afterwards. The prisoner who left this description of being tortured in 1597 was the Jesuit priest, John Gerard, who was being persuaded to disclose the routes by which letters were being brought into England from Jesuits in the Low Countries and Spain.

The manacles in this form were adopted fairly late in the reign of Elizabeth I, principally against Jesuits felt to be a danger to the Queen. Henry Walpole, a Jesuit missionary priest, was allegedly subjected to the manacles 14 times, causing him to lose the use of his fingers for a while, and permanently ruining his hands. Fellow Catholics claimed that Walpole's torture had been so brutal that it was moved to a private cell, to avoid causing widespread outrage.

John Gerard was tortured twice. Despite the agonising pain he resisted answering any but the simplest questions: a surviving transcript of his examination contains almost no information. Gerard later escaped by climbing along a rope from the Cradle Tower to the wharf, from where a boat carried him to safety.

The Jesuit priest John Gerard (1564–1637) being suspended by manacles in the White Tower. Though tortured further, Gerard gave little away and later actually escaped from the Tower.

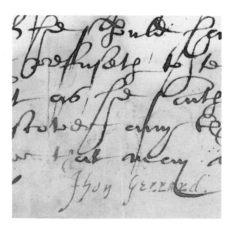

John Gerard's signature from his interrogation statement. Gerard later recorded that throughout his ordeal his warder continually urged him to spare himself further suffering by answering the questions put to him.

Rudolph Hess was one of the last state prisoners to be held at the Tower.

Rudolf Hess
(1894–1987)

PRISONER: 1941

Rudolf Hess, the son of a wealthy German merchant, was born in Alexandria, Egypt. He joined the German Army in August 1914 and served in the 1st Bavarian Infantry Regiment during the First World War. He was one of the first to join the Nazi party, in 1920, and soon became a devoted follower of Adolf Hitler. In 1933 he was appointed Deputy Führer and Minister without Portfolio.

On 10 May 1941, Hess made a solo flight from Augsburg, Bavaria, to Scotland where he crash-landed his plane, parachuting into fields outside Glasgow. The purpose of his mission remains one of the great unresolved mysteries of the Second World War.

Some suggest that his intention, with or without Hitler's permission, was to negotiate peace between Germany and the United Kingdom and to unite against the Soviet Union; others believe he was lured to Britain by the British Secret Intelligence Service.

Hess was taken to the Tower of London on 17 May 1941 and was lodged under the tightest security in the King's House (now the Queen's House). During his brief stay he signed a piece of notepaper for one of his guards, which still survives in the Tower club. After four days of interrogation, he was removed from the Tower and spent the rest of the war as a prisoner at Mytchett Place in Surrey. At the

Nuremberg Trials of 1946, he was sentenced to life imprisonment in Spandau, West Berlin, where he became known as 'Prisoner Number Seven', although he was the sole occupant of the prison after 1966.

Hess's death is also shrouded in mystery. On 17 August 1987, he was found hanging from an electrical cord. Possibly he committed suicide; others suggest that, at the age of 93, he would have been too old and frail to do this himself and may have received some assistance – or even been murdered. There is also a theory that the 'Hess' incarcerated in Spandau for 40 years was an imposter and that the real Hess was executed in 1941.

Nicholas Owen (d 1606), a Catholic priest, being suspended from manacles with rocks tied to his feet. Owen died under torture though his gaolers claimed he killed himself.

The torturers and interrogators

A certain amount of information has survived about the individuals who actually tortured prisoners in the Tower. There is an important distinction between those who operated the instruments and those who questioned the prisoners during each session. The sources have far more to say about the second group but the identity of the torturers themselves is fairly clear. It was the warders of the Tower, under the command of the Lieutenant, who saw to the physical business of torture. As a proclamation of 1583 explained, 'the Queen's servants, the warders, whose office and act it is to handle the rack, were ever, by those that attended the examinations, specially charged to use it in as charitable a manner as such a thing might be'.

The interrogations themselves were carried out by two or three commissioners, usually including at least one law officer, such as the royal attorney or solicitor. One of these, Thomas Norton, MP and Recorder of London, who was frequently requested to interrogate prisoners in the late 1570s

Sir William Waad (1546–1623), Lieutenant of the Tower from 1603 to 1613. Waad was in charge of the Tower during Walter Ralegh's lengthy imprisonment and Guy Fawkes's interrogation. Ralegh called him 'that beast Waad'.

Norton died in 1584. Within a few years, he had been replaced in Roman Catholic pamphlets by a new demon, Richard Topcliffe, who operated as an interrogator all over England. Topcliffe was not a law officer and appears to have carried out much of the torturing in person. On one infamous occasion, he tortured the Jesuit Robert Southwell in his house by hanging him from the manacles. He then went out of the house and forgot about the prisoner, who was only rescued from death by the action of one of Topcliffe's servants, who caused him to be let down.

While Topcliffe and Norton took to their jobs with something verging on relish, other officers found the duty an unpleasant one. Gerard later heard that Sir Richard Berkeley resigned as Lieutenant, not wishing to be involved in torture again. Sir Thomas Smith, who had been requested by Elizabeth I to torture two servants of the Duke of Norfolk in 1571, later wrote: 'I do most humbly crave my revocation from this unpleasant and painful toil. I assure you I would not wish to be one of Homer's Gods... I had rather be one of the least shades in the Elysian fields'.

Torture in the Tower

This book has examined the prisoners in the Tower in isolation from the events that placed them there. Before leaving the subject, a word needs to be said about the wider context in which torture was practised. This is another instance in which the popular idea and the historical reality are somewhat different.

and early 1580s, has left a number of documents describing the process and reason for torturing prisoners. Norton's radical Protestant views and the rigour with which he interrogated Catholic priests gave him the nickname 'Norton the Rackmaster' (to which he objected, pointing out that it was the Lieutenant's men who operated the rack). While under house arrest for outspoken behaviour in 1582, he wrote several documents justifying the torture of the Jesuits as an essential matter of state security. He protested that no one was ever questioned about matters of religion, but only to discover evidence of plots against the Queen and insisted that torture was always carried out slowly, 'unwillingly' and with frequent statements of how the prisoner could be spared, simply by answering the questions. Under such circumstances, Norton claimed, torture was unpleasant but necessary and the victims had only themselves to blame.

In the mid-16th century, most of the cases of torture were related to crimes such as robbery and murder and the object of torture was to force the prisoner to confess his own guilt. These instances of torture relied on good circumstantial evidence that the prisoner was guilty and, by modern standards of proof, were obviously unjust, since victims of torture can often be made to confess to anything. On at least one occasion, in 1588, that of Tristram Winslade, discovered on board a Spanish ship and thought to be a traitor, the prisoner was racked and later discovered to be innocent: he had been brought on board the ship against his will, and was released. As Elizabeth I's reign progressed, torture was used increasingly in cases of treason, particularly in connection with alleged Catholic plots against her. In many of these instances, the victims were deemed to be guilty already, and now the object was not to extract a confession, so much as to gather information about conspirators, safe-houses, the routes of letters and so on. In the reign of James I (1603–25), Sir Francis Bacon wrote, 'in the highest cases of treasons, torture is used for discovery, and not for evidence'.

It is no coincidence that the period covered by this chapter, from the mid-16th to the mid-17th century, was a period of religious upheaval in England, from Henry VIII's declaration of his own Supremacy over the Church, through to the shifting tones of Protestant authority under the Stuarts. Insecurity over the religious settlement was ever-present, sometimes translated into fears that an invasion or a coup d'état would lead to violent change. In such a climate, as for example in the reign of Elizabeth I from 1570 onwards (when she was excommunicated by the Pope), it became possible to see all members of another religion as potential traitors. In such times of national emergency, it was claimed, the government needed to use every available method to protect itself and thus the use of torture to gather information became a matter of state policy.

Whereas the popular image of torture is that the victims were forced to admit their religious views and then induced to convert to the other side, there is no good evidence for this in England; torture was a matter of state security, not religious creed. But we should be careful not to separate them too much. Motives are notoriously hard to detect centuries after the event, but it seems likely that some of the torturers and councillors, Catholic or Protestant, were driven by a desire to protect their own religion from challenge, as well as to secure the throne. On the side of the prisoners and their supporters at large, religion was certainly their main possible reason for resisting their interrogators. Torture showed the gaolers to be no more than persecutors, while they themselves could take strength in knowing that they were imitating Christ and the Apostles, who had been imprisoned, suffered and died. Though some conspiracies were stopped, religious uncertainty prevailed and torture strengthened the resolve of those outside the Tower to continue their struggle. To that end, the experiment can be called a failure.

View towards Traitors' Gate, the traditional river entrance associated with traitors. By the late 16th century torture was commonly used on religious prisoners during interrogation at the Tower.

Index

Illustrations

Abbreviations: b = bottom, c = centre, l = left, r = right, t = top

Further reading

Ainsworth, W H. *The Tower of London*, London, 1840

Bayley, J. *The History and Antiquities of the Tower of London*, London, 1821

Dasent, J R (ed). *Acts of the Privy Council*, especially volumes 1–30

Hammond, P. 'Epitome of England's history', *Royal Armouries Yearbook*, Volume 4, 1999, pp 144–74

Harrison, B A. *A Tudor Journal. The Diary of a Priest in the Tower*, London, 2000

Heath, J. *Torture and English Law*, Westport, 1982

Impey, E and Parnell, G. *The Tower of London. The Official Illustrated History*, Merrell Publishers, 2000

Keay, A. *The Earl of Essex: The life and death of a Tudor traitor*, Historic Royal Palaces, 2001

Langbein, J. *Torture and the Law of Proof*, Chicago, 1977

Parnell, G. *The Tower Past and Present*, Stroud, 1998

Strong, R. *And When did you last see your father? The Victorian Painter and British History*, London, 1978

Cover, main image: *Prisoners' inscriptions in the Beauchamp Tower.*
Front cover portraits (left to right): *Princess Elizabeth, Henry VI, Sir Walter Ralegh, Henry Laurens, Rudolf Hess.*

Back cover portraits (left to right): *John the Good, Anne Boleyn, Thomas Coningsby, Gerhard Glattes, Henry Wriothesley, 3rd Earl of Southampton.*

Page 4: *The White Tower.*

Page 78: *Engraving of Edward Oldcorne (1561–1606) being racked. Oldcorne, a Jesuit priest, was imprisoned in the Tower in 1605 on suspicion of being involved in the Gunpowder Plot. He was later executed.*

Page 80: *The block, axe and executioner's mask, from The Illustrated London News, 1883.*

Acknowledgements

Sebastian Edwards would like to thank his former colleague,
Jeremy Ashbee, and Bridget Clifford at the Royal Armouries for
their generous assistance in researching his chapter. Much
credit must also go to Peter Hammond for his seminal article
('Epitome of England's history', *Royal Armouries Yearbook*,
Volume 4, 1999, pp 144–74) on the Tower as a visitor
attraction, which deserves to be much more widely known.

Case studies by: Brett Dolman, Sebastian Edwards,
Chris Gidlow, Clare Murphy, David Souden, Jane Spooner,
Lucy Worsley
Edited by: Clare Murphy and David Souden

Designed by: Star Design
Printed by: City Digital Limited

Published by Historic Royal Palaces
Hampton Court Palace
Surrey
KT8 9AU

ISBN 1 873993 45 5

Historic Royal Palaces is a registered charity (no. 1068852).

www.hrp.org.uk

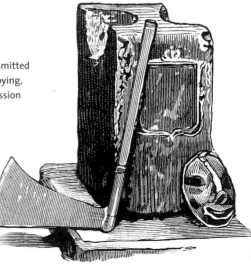